# Rethinking the Tropical House

13. 04. 04

# Rethinking the Tropical House
# 20 Years of RT+Q Architects

Text by Luo Jingmei
Forewords by Rene Tan and TK Quek

With 430 illustrations

Cover photograph: Spice Terraces © Masano Kawana

First published in the United Kingdom in 2023 by
Thames & Hudson Ltd, 181A High Holborn, London WC1V 7QX

*Rethinking the Tropical House: 20 Years of RT+Q Architects* © 2023
RT+Q Architects Pte Ltd

Texts by Luo Jingmei

'Unique is RT+Q' © 2023 Erwin Viray
'A Practice at the Intersection' © 2023 Chan Sau Yan, Sonny
'A Counterintuitive Partnership' © 2023 Robert Powell
'Modern Spirit, Classical Heart' © 2023 Lillian Tay
'Equilibrio Perfetto (Perfect Balance)' © 2023 Alexander Wong
'Composing a Creative Practice' © 2023 Mok Wei Wei
'Counter-Intuitive Design' © 2023 Kelley Cheng
For illustrations, please see the Photographic Credits on p. 342

RT+Q Book Team: Koh Sock Mui, Liane Ee,
    Nazirah Adam and Chommanard Chumduang
Forewords by Rene Tan and TK Quek
Design by H55
Edited by Justin Zhuang

British Library Cataloguing-in-Publication Data
A catalogue record for this book is available from the British Library

ISBN   978-0-500-02596-3

Printed in China by RR Donnelley

MIX
Paper | Supporting
responsible forestry
FSC
www.fsc.org    FSC® C144853

Be the first to know about our new releases,
exclusive content and author events by visiting
**thamesandhudson.com**
**thamesandhudsonusa.com**
**thamesandhudson.com.au**

# CONTENTS

# Foreword

—Rene Tan

When I was reminded I should write something for this monograph, my intuition was to expound on views about design, the making of architecture and how TK and I have contributed to this practice over the past twenty years.

However, counterintuition prevailed.

Who wants to hear more about architecture, when the images in this book would do it anyway?!

Architecture is elusive, an enigma. The more we try to describe or explain it, the further it drifts away. Like certain things, it is best left unexplained – especially the ones that we ourselves create.

I also learned in music school that good conductors always know when to let the orchestra play by itself. So don't over-design.

Instead, I will share non-architectural events that have shaped the works presented here – and reveal the carnage of counterintuitive collisions that made this book possible.

### Music

I have often described myself as an 'accidental architect' because I set out in college to be a pianist. An injury to my right ring finger curtailed aspirations of a serious concert career; and playing left-hand repertory only was never enough. Realizing I could draw a bit, I started taking drawing and architecture courses, and graduated with a double major in music and architecture – eventually going to graduate school for the latter. But music never left me. Having studied both architecture and music, I often ask myself (and get asked too) how they are similar – and different.

Ever since music writer Johann Wolfgang von Goethe mused 'architecture is frozen music', scholars and students alike have wondered about their similarities. Very often, words such as 'structure', 'rhythm' and 'form' come to bear. For instance, one can say, quite rightly, that the music of Johann Sebastian Bach is very 'tectonic and architectural'. That is because its Baroque rhythms are strict and structured in the way it holds the 'edifice' together. You can even measure rationally the length of both music and architecture. This is only one type of 'similarity' that can be drawn between music and architecture, but we won't discuss this further.

Instead, it is precisely the 'irrational' in music and architecture that fascinates me. Both are art forms and, as such, contain the unpredictable and are open to chance. For instance, I particularly like music by the composer Sergei Prokofiev and the rock group Queen for their wit. Both have unpredictable and surrealist elements. Prokofiev's Violin Concerto No. 2, for example, fascinates me. Just when you think the phrasing is coming to an end, Prokofiev does the opposite. There is a sense of 'miscarriage' in his music that keeps it interesting and fresh. His Piano Concerto No. 2, likewise, thrills me every time I listen to it. The juxtaposition between the lyrical and the discordant is 'bizarre'. I never tire from engaging with Prokofiev.

Similarly, *Bohemian Rhapsody* by Queen is 'rhapsodic' and memorable because it takes every rule of a rhapsody to its logical conclusion – not unlike John Cage and silences in *4'33"*. The confounding rhythms and shifts in mood capture the human condition unlike most other music. Igor Stravinsky's *The Rite of Spring* does the same thing too. It is witty and its violent shifts in tempo and rhythm surprise and inspire. Stravinsky was not out to write music, nor a ballet; he was looking to capture a moment.

These elements in music have shaped the diversity of our work and taught us several lessons. To use our counterintuition and to never be afraid to put the right thing in the wrong place – just two of the things that architects can borrow from music.

### Football

I have often said that if I weren't an architect, I would be a football historian of sorts.

What fascinates me about football is how similar it is to architecture – the management and liberation of space. I believe that architecture is not about the 'creation' of spaces because you really cannot: space already exists anyway in various guises. But what we can do is to free it of encumbrances and let space be what it wants to be.

I watch a lot of football and have read a lot ranging from the best team management to strategic play formations in the game. 'Total football', largely an invention of the Dutch teams of the 1970s, is founded on the well-known concept by which every player can play in any position. What is less known is that it is also predicated on what a team does when they don't have the ball – they mark, control and liberate space. Very often, we hear commentators say 'He has got acres of space around him' or 'He has the whole pitch to himself', and so on. Like architecture, football is about making good spatial compositions to control territory, to overcome challenges – and to score.

There are books and debates about the team formations of 4-3-3 or 4-4-2. This is football language and codifications of how to manage space. What is interesting is how formations can readjust themselves depending on the opponents the team plays. Flexibility is important to both football and architecture. Architects too need constantly to reposition themselves owing to the vagaries of site, clients and needs. Especially so these days.

As a great mentor of mine once said, the making of architecture is like cooking – for example, like boiling soup. You stir the pot, throw in ingredients, taste it as you progress, keep stirring until you get it right. This little piece of advice has never left me.

So, don't think like an architect. Think like a chef. In this instance, at least.

*I would like to acknowledge the following:*
*...my mother, whom I have never seen buying anything for herself; my dad, for introducing me to art and jazz, and their ineffable beauty;*
*...TK for his collegiality and wisdom; Jes for being a colleague from the ice age;*
*...Lara for unlocking the mysteries of opera and explaining the human condition to me and for reinvigorating my interest in THE GAME;*
*...and Woei Woei for showing me how to live.*

—TK Quek

The year was 1970. The graduation ceremony of the then University of Singapore was held at the former National Theatre. As the four graduates including myself were called up to be awarded our Bachelor of Architecture degrees, the other graduands turned around, looked at us in wonderment and asked: 'Huh? Where is the architecture department on the campus?'

In fact, there was none.

We were educated in a very modest building on the former Singapore Polytechnic campus at Prince Edward Road. Unbeknown to many, the polytechnic's architecture programme had been transferred to the university in 1969. Prior to this, the programme established in 1958 had already been conferring professional diplomas on many architects who would later become outstanding pioneer professionals in Singapore, including the likes of Tay Kheng Soon and Wee Chwee Heng.

Immediately upon graduation, I was conscripted into the army for National Service, like all Singaporean males. After going through basic military training, I was seconded to the Defence Department in the Public Works Department, then the government agency in charge of developing public buildings and infrastructure in Singapore. I was fortunate to serve the rest of my service period executing architecture projects for the Ministry of Defence.

My next architectural office was at the local practice of James Ferrie & Partners, where I had the good fortune to meet colleagues such as Ian Lander, a competent and dedicated Australian architect. Along with my boss Lee Seng Loong, Ian and I worked on a limited competition design proposal for the Sabah Foundation Building (Yayasan Sabah) in Kota Kinabalu, Malaysia. Our winning design was a cylindrical building with a concrete core and a glass curtain wall held up by cable structures, which we worked closely with Joe Huang of Arup Associates to realize.

At that time, there were only two cable-suspended buildings in the world. One was in South Africa and the other was the Westcoast Transmission Building (now the Qube) in Vancouver, Canada. Thanks to the generosity and encouragement of my bosses, I visited the latter. My career now took a different turn as Vancouver seduced me, with its beautiful natural setting of sea and mountain. I decided to move to the city, as I wanted to gain some international experience. I secured a position with a mid-sized architectural firm, where I worked on various projects over several years.

After six years in Vancouver, I returned to Singapore and visited my former firm. To my pleasant surprise, James Ferrie made me an offer of work again, which I could not refuse. That was how I returned to Singapore for good. It was while working at the firm in 1982 that talented Thai architect Pisit Villavong and I entered an architectural competition for a new clubhouse to be built at Bukit Timah along Sime Road. This was for the Singapore Island Country Club. We worked tirelessly and with great enthusiasm. Our proposal won first prize among fifty-two submissions from countries across the Association of Southeast Asian Nations (ASEAN). It was then that I felt a very strong sense of professional satisfaction. It was also midway through the construction of this project that I felt ready to strike out on my own. I told my employers of my decision to leave and start my own architectural practice. Quek Associates was thus formed. Here, I practised for about a decade.

In 1990, my wife and I were in the USA, accompanied by fourteen-year-old Jonathan, to try to enrol my older son, Calvin, into the Syracuse School of Architecture. I was told that I would meet a young professor from my part of the world, who turned out to be Rene Tan. We had a very fruitful meeting, and it was during our enthusiastic conversation that I expressed quietly to Rene that he should return to Asia, as architects in the region were very busy with new work. A couple of years later, he moved to Singapore and joined a friend's firm. Around 2003, Rene approached me and proposed that we start a new firm together. That was how RT+Q Architects originated.

The firm started with nothing but our enthusiasm and hope. We had just three staff and no clients, and we cracked our brains in thinking of ways to reach out to acquaintances for jobs. During the early days, I recall picking Rene up at his house in the wee hours of the morning at 5.00 a.m. to drive to Kuala Lumpur, Malaysia, to meet potential clients. We lined up several meetings throughout the day before driving all the way back to Singapore. I vividly recall crossing through Immigration many times after midnight, feeling totally exhausted.

At the beginning, Rene and I often discussed how our office should be. One of our guiding principles is that 'we must create good architecture, have fun and make a little money'. Over the years, we have kept the office smallish to remain close to our assignments. It has also allowed us to stay efficient and work intimately with people. Our staff can be described as young, energetic and self-motivated. We try to extract their best qualities while also enthusing them with creative ideas and more mundane, but equally important, affairs such as contract and project management.

My fervent hope is that we have imparted our skills and knowledge to these young and enthusiastic architects. It will hopefully inspire and motivate them to improve their architecture skills, and ultimately be better than their bosses at RT+Q.

# A Journey of Rediscovering

—Luo Jingmei

A building is a world within a world.
Buildings that personify places of worship,
Or of home, or of other institutions of man
Must be true to their nature.
– Louis Kahn[1]

The story is a familiar one in local design circles and media: while enrolling his older son in the architecture school of Syracuse University, New York, a Singaporean architect is introduced to a Malaysian architect. Years later, they end up forming a partnership in Singapore that becomes known for its beautiful, well-resolved houses. The first architect is Quek Tse Kwang (fondly addressed by most as TK) and the second is Rene Tan. They founded RT+Q Architects in 2003.

It has been many decades since that serendipitous meeting. The partnership is now twenty years old and the firm had completed more than 170 projects at the time of this book's completion – most of them single-family dwellings comprising a mix of terraced and semi-detached houses, bungalows and shophouses. The firm has also designed some condominiums, small offices, stage sets and even tombstones. In the sea of 'modern' houses in Singapore, RT+Q Architects' works stand out for their clarity of form, considered composition and elegant detailing. The dwellings are artful but also logical and efficacious in dealing with tropical conditions. Within the medley of tempered forms are instances of drama and originality that lend surprise and delight to the quotidian occurrences of domestic life. The ability to create a discernible genius loci (spirit of place) stems from the conceptual rigour grounding the projects, derived from classical and modernist architectural theory, as well as a persistent rethinking of architectural tropes and understanding of context.

The firm is located in a shophouse in Mosque Street, Chinatown, with TK's and Rene's different responsibilities clearly defined. TK works together with the staff on administrative, contractual and project management issues, while Rene leads the design aspects. The clear division between these two roles plays a big part in making the partnership a successful and long-lasting one, despite the partners' twenty-year age difference. Both already had illustrious backgrounds before they became partners.

Born in 1944, TK decided to enrol in the Singapore Polytechnic to study architecture simply because of his adept drawing skills. 'I guess if I didn't do architecture, I would work for an advertising company, or maybe become a pilot, because the uniform attracted me,' he quips. In his third year, the course morphed into a five-year Bachelor of Arts degree when the architecture course came under the National University of Singapore. TK did his mandatory year of internship at Design Partnership (now DP Architects) and Architects Team 3. At the former, he learned the ropes of design from pioneer architects including Tay Kheng Soon, who was part of the team that produced modernist icons such as People's Park Complex and Golden Mile Complex. At the latter, veteran architect Lim Chong Keat,[2] who was one of TK's lecturers and whose firm produced the futuristic Jurong Town Hall, provided guidance.

'During my internship at Architects Team 3, I drew windows for three months. I remember Chong Keat said to us, "If you want to do architecture, learn to build a brick wall first",' TK recalls in one of the lessons he passes down to his staff. After completing his degree, he worked at SLH Partners and James Ferrie & Partners. A trip to Vancouver to see the Westcoast Transmission Building (now a residence called Qube) – then one of only two 'suspended' buildings in the world that was top-hung from cables – as research for the design of the Sabah Foundation at James Ferrie resulted in his staying to work for Canadian architecture firm Armour + Blewett. After five years, he returned to James Ferrie's office.

Quek Associates was started when TK was forty, in the very shophouse that houses RT+Q's offices today. It was ten years later that he met Rene at Syracuse University. TK was struck by the latter's beautiful drawings for a competition and immediately acknowledged his superior design skills. When Rene suggested a partnership sometime after returning to Singapore, TK welcomed the idea. 'I thought, maybe we could try. After all, I was at the age where I should retire but suddenly there was this new opportunity with an architect who is twenty years younger than me.' He decided to give it five years. Happily, this has turned into twenty.

Rene was born in Terengganu, Malaysia, in 1964, but grew up in Penang. His schoolteacher father introduced him to jazz. 'He played the trumpet. Music moved me,' says Rene, who took up the piano. He started studying music at Yale but in his second year, he developed tendonitis in his hands, which affected his piano playing. He eventually graduated with a Bachelor of Arts (Magna cum Laude), majoring in both music and architecture – 'two labour-intensive fields that nearly killed me,' he says, only half in jest. A Master of Architecture from Princeton followed, where he was awarded the Suzanne Kolarik Underwood Prize for design.

His schooling greatly influenced his approach to architecture. 'At Yale, my mentors were Vincent Scully and Kent Bloomer. There I learned about the humanities and the value of history. At Princeton, where I was mentored by Michael Graves, Ralph Lerner and Anthony Ames, I learned

23 April 20

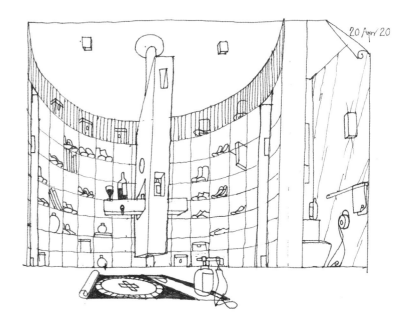

20 Apr 20

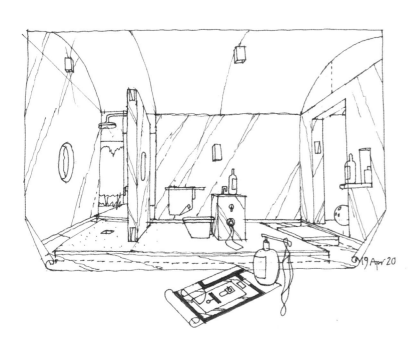

19 Apr 20

26 Apr 20

about architecture history and theory. Ames is an avid admirer of Le Corbusier, and it shows in his designs and paintings. I admired the beauty of his plans and the clarity of his forms, and liked the way he presented his work with reference to precedents,' Rene recalls on the American architect. Rene himself later became an educator, teaching at the University of California, Berkeley, and New York's Syracuse University (where he also conducted a course in 'Descriptive Geometry'). For him, drawings are essential tools of communication. He leans towards a multitude of mediums, from sketches and paintings to Choisy diagrams, which showcase the relationship of the plans to the volumes of spaces they generate – a particularly effective way to convey the drama of spaces.

After graduation, he worked for Lerner from 1990 to 1994, 'where I remain grateful for [learning] everything one needs to know about becoming a teacher and an architect', he says. In 1996, he came to Singapore and worked at SCDA Architects, to which he remains indebted for a solid introduction to tropical architecture. Seven years later, Rene and TK teamed up. The partnership has remained strong after twenty years, no doubt thanks to mutual admiration, trust and respect. 'The success of RT+Q Architects is based on a sound partnership. I work with the architects on contractual and administrative matters, and Rene does the design. It's a good relationship,' says TK. 'Rene tries very hard himself. He doesn't tell the staff to design by themselves and then sit down and have a coffee.

He is very inquisitive in his own way and always wants to try something new.' Rene returns the compliments: 'We balance each other out. TK is a gentleman most of all, and that's all that really matters.' They run the firm in an egalitarian way and share their expertise without any sense of the Architect's ego in place. Rene describes the firm as 'a mid-sized architecture firm in Singapore comprising some eleven equally "weighted" colleagues (like a football team) and well-rounded individuals who contribute towards the work, the identity and the culture of all the office'. Credit is always given to colleagues, particularly when a project has won a prize – a frequent occurrence in the firm's twenty-year existence, including local awards from the Singapore Institute of Architecture and the Urban Redevelopment Authority, as well as overseas accolades from the likes of the Chicago Athenaeum International Architecture Awards.

'We want to teach the younger architects that they can also make it,' says TK, referring to the belief that his architects should develop independence and confidence in leading their projects. There is a quote from TK that Rene often cites like an office motto: 'Let's do good architecture, have fun, and make some money' – in that order, which speaks for the palpable sense of camaraderie in the office.

Through the years, Rene has consistently incorporated academia into his practice. There are annual trips, such as to Switzerland, Greece, India and Italy, to discover the world; in Rome, Rene becomes a guide to history as

they experience masterpieces by Francesco Borromini and Gian Lorenzo Bernini in the flesh. Alongside speaking at symposiums and participating as a juror at the World Architecture Festival, Rene also ropes his staff in to studio courses he runs at the National University of Singapore (NUS) and the Singapore University of Technology and Design (SUTD). His role in the office is akin to a studio master in architecture school, as he goes energetically from table to table commenting on design resolutions and holding crits rather than being tied to a fixed seat. Colleagues join him on weekly Saturday site visits to selected projects.

The firm's altruistic attitude towards architecture has also sprouted in the travelling exhibition of the collection of models of Le Corbusier buildings created by interns over the years. These were first presented in October 2021 in Singapore during Archifest at the Alliance Française, and then at NUS, SUTD and the National Design Centre. By the end of 2024, the exhibition will have travelled to at least twenty-eight cities, including Jakarta, Barcelona and London. The generosity of the partners also extends outside the firm: in 2017, they conceived the RT+Q Rome Prize, a monetary award granted to one BSc in Architecture & Sustainable Design student who has excelled at SUTD.

To think counterintuitively, to put the 'right thing in the wrong place', has been Rene's mantra from the start, grounded in the Vitruvian principles of *firmitas*, *utilitas* and *venustas* (strength, utility and beauty). This results in inventive architecture. 'Every house, every project is an opportunity to create something different, as long as RT+Q's core values of proportion, scale and craft are preserved,' says Rene.

While he plays music for recreation these days, his musical background has been a strong influence in his thinking about architecture; architects Frank Lloyd Wright and Paul Rudolph were similar in that aspect. He often finds parallels between the two disciplines. 'Each project is an attempt to find a rhythm of space and a melody of proportion that seek to bring chaos to order,' he has said in an interview when he was acclaimed the Designer of the Year at Singapore's President*s Design Award in 2016. As in music, each piece works to address an identified challenge or 'thesis', such as the light, the terrain or the programme (a term referring to the spatial organization in

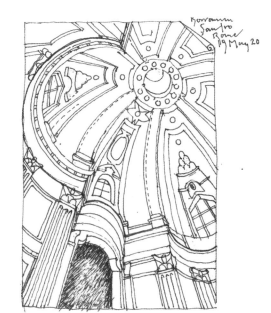

a building). 'You know Chopin's études? He wrote twenty-seven;[3] one is about octaves; another is about black keys. Every étude is about an aspect of piano playing. So I hope, in a similar way, every project we do will address a certain aspect of the making of architecture.[4] Even if there's no obvious challenge, we create one. This gives our work a purpose, an intention, so that we don't design for the sake of designing,' says Rene.

This plays out literally in House in Three Movements (pp. 70–77), where he segmented the massing into three distinct blocks (like in three-part symphonies or sonatas) down the plot's depth, each clad in a different material. In rethinking the semi-detached house model, he offset the blocks from both sides, reducing the already tight square metrage even further but overall producing superior interiors with additional light and ventilation, as well as the clear reading of form. One of the firm's early significant works was House at Holland (pp. 14–23). The windows were set in, creating overhangs that protect the interiors from harsh sunlight or rain. At the same time, the language was minimal and modern, with a fluid, abstracted form that marked on the local residential design scene a rethinking of tropical house design when most at that time were producing nondescript variations of the modernist box or the Balinese type with stone walls and pitched roofs. Rene's own second home, House at Watten (pp. 24–29), presented a similar way of rethinking tropical house design. Simply by skewing the plan, he created courtyards that made the house porous and connected. The all-white structure offered no attempt to recede into the background, instead celebrating the plasticity of architecture through its strong, sculptural presence that broke out of the modernist box's predictability. Subsequent projects that further employ this abstract lexicon include House with a Sanctum (pp. 204–217), Spice Terraces (pp. 280–293) and the buildings in the Sentul East development (pp. 88–99).

The firm's receptiveness to new approaches and influences from the longer continuum of architecture resulted in a segment of the portfolio featuring homes with monolithic pitched roof forms, such as the Svarga Residence in Bali (pp. 102–113), House with Bridges (pp. 144–153), House with Shadows (pp. 174–187) and House with Gables (pp. 248–259). They take the opposite approach of abstracting the domestic house form by returning to the familiar and basic silhouette of a child's naive drawing of a house. Marc-Antoine Laugier's 1753 thesis on 'the Primitive Hut' extolling structural rationalism provided much insight. Alongside these experiments, the firm continues to adapt the modernist box diagram to suit its tropical environs with screens, extended roof eaves and well-ventilated plans, such as the extensions in House at Cable (pp. 50–59), the Shorefront condominium development in Penang (pp. 78–87) and TK's own house – the Art Collector's House (pp. 132–143), which he designed with his younger son, Jonathan Quek, who joined the firm in 2006.

Although Rene highlights that the sensibilities were always there from the start, he has been increasingly looking to Baroque architecture for guidance, albeit more for its spatial devices than ornamentation. 'We want to rethink aesthetics and form. Modern architecture, when misinterpreted, can rob architecture of its richness. Baroque architecture restores meaning to architecture,' he says. Architecture should not only be functional but also provide beauty found in sensual encounters. 'Whether it is a double-volume height or roundish space, all our houses try to embody the formal drama of Baroque buildings, such as the atrium in TK's house, the ovoid guest bathroom in House of the Twins (pp. 164–173) or the shoe cabinet in Spice Terraces. Such grandiose gestures are not just reserved for churches and chapels, but also employed for normal houses in the tropics,' Rene says. It sets the wheel turning for a new category of works in the firm's oeuvre, which has up till now been categorized into three overarching and sometimes overlapping classifications of Abstraction (playful experiments with form and function), the Primitive Hut (explorations of classical ideas of dwelling) and Tropical Modernism (adapting the modernist box for the tropics).

The firm's approach is similar regardless of scale and programme, as shown in projects featured in this book such as The Capers (pp. 88–99) condominium in the Sentul East development or the multi-purpose Sentul Pavilion (pp. 300–311). One is the house model writ large; the other is a condensed version. 'The towers are conceived as tropical homes stacked up in the air with balconies and sky gardens. The Sentul Pavilion is essentially a glasshouse that utilizes natural vent circulation with a volume high enough for hot air to rise, stay and vent out,' Rene says.

Within the firmament of domestic tropical architecture in Singapore and the region, RT+Q Architects continues to create interesting and assertive narratives that are rooted in place and time. Commonplace components become instances of delight, and rudimentary forms are elevated to art with the articulation of an edge or the unexpected placement of parts. 'Architecture is about discovery, telling and retelling stories,' Rene once quipped. In my investigation and personal experience of so many of the firm's works, I have found this to be true.

Endnotes

1    Louis I. Kahn, *Conversations with Students: Architecture at Rice 26* (New York, Princeton Architectural Press, 1969), 28.

2    Datuk Seri Lim Chong Keat is regarded as one of the most important architects of Singapore and Malaysia who worked in the modern tradition. He helped to establish Singapore's first school of architecture, where he also taught students such as Tay Kheng Soon. Lim co-founded the Malayan Architects Co-partnership (MAC), which had offices in Kuala Lumpur and Singapore. It won the design competition for the Singapore Conference Hall, regarded as among the country's greatest works of modern architecture. After the partnership ended, Lim founded Architects Team 3.

3    Frédéric Chopin wrote twenty-seven études but only twenty-four are commonly played.

4    Luo Jingmei, 'Well Composed' (*Cubes Indesign*, Issue 65, December/January 2013/2014), 75.

# Unique is RT+Q

—Erwin Viray

'RT+Q is unique', is how I started another essay that I wrote earlier. In this one, with a lighter tone, I would like to explore what is unique about RT+Q Architects.

It is unique in its multiples. It is unique in having Rene Tan with his vibrant energetic character. It is unique in having Quek Tse Kwang (TK) with his calm and steady disposition. These are balanced by the youthful and measured character of the young director Jonathan Quek and associates such as Koh Sock Mui, Koh Kai Li and Tiw Pek Hong, plus the student-like enthusiasm and energy of the other members of the studio.

RT+Q is unique in being like an architectural studio in school: energetic, enthusiastic, curious and with a strong sense of learning from history. I have observed its members run studios, and the rigour of having very organized lessons and timelines comes through. They also provide a good and strategic distribution of assignments to study, analysing architectural precedents and imagining something for the future.

I have enjoyed travelling with the studio on trips to Venice and Paris to appreciate and discover the works of architects such as Andrea Palladio and Le Corbusier, as well as the life in these cities. It is not discovering just architecture, but the life that surrounds it – lessons that are translated into the works of RT+Q. Be it in their houses, housing projects, theatre sets or even a tombstone, the past is present in the conscious tradition of being mindful of geometry, proportions and composition – all fundamental principles in creating architecture. In the choice of materials, there is also a great concern for and study of what is appropriate in a particular context in these different scales and typologies of projects. The details of RT+Q's works are fascinating for the lessons they offer on the ideas of precedents by the likes of Le Corbusier, Carlo Scarpa and other masters of modern architecture. Each offers a new interpretation of the details and fragments of memories that elicit joyful thoughts and open new visions.

It is interesting to ask Rene about the architects he respects and who have influenced him, as he brings the lessons from them and interactions with them back to the studio to create new possibilities. I asked Rene about the following architects' influences, to which he responded:

Le Corbusier
    the combination of bold and free
        concrete forms
    the free plan
    the precision of geometry and order
    the use of colour
    the beauty of light e.g. Convent of
        La Tourette

Scarpa
    the attention to details and materials

Palladio
    the proportion and scale of his façades
    the regulating lines
    the Pythagorean dictum of the relation
        of music, numerical ratios and
        architecture
    lessons from art historian Rudolf Wittkower

Filippo Brunelleschi
    structural clarity and rhythm

Gian Lorenzo Bernini
    plasticity of sculptural forms
    false perspectives

Francesco Borromini
    strong Baroque formal gestures
    façades that sculpt and shape space

Michael Graves
    the architect as an artist
    the importance of a good plan and the
        values learned at Princeton University
    'The Lesson of Rome' and the definition of
        interior space

    the 'architecture of lines' in his early
        houses, e.g. Benacerraf and
        Hanselmann houses
    the formal clarity and complexity of the
        New York Five

Ralph Lerner
    the discipline and rigours of architecture
    the politics of teaching

Anthony Ames
    the architect as a 'gentleman'
    the architect as an artist
    the design methodology of quoting
        precedents in his works
    the attention to drawing and the
        portraying of 'the good life' that his
        architecture aims for
    his beautiful paintings
    his American Academy in Rome legacy

Werner Seligmann
    passion and love for teaching
    the architect as the cultured gentleman
    his lessons on Le Corbusier and Frank
        Lloyd Wright
    the Syracuse curriculum that combined
        the best of modernity and Renaissance
        that I inherited teaching there between
        1994 to 1996

And in addition, Tadao Ando, who I believe is the greatest living architect today.

Obviously, Le Corbusier is the root of all evil, or the good, shall we say, in laying the foundations for Rene's appreciation of the architectural project and the city. We can see Le Corbusier's five points – pilotis, free plan, free design of the façade, horizontal windows and the roof garden – already being tested in the works of the High Renaissance architects and artists such as Palladio, Bernini, Borromini and others. Seligmann was also a great influence on Rene after their meeting at

Syracuse University when the latter joined the faculty. Between 1951 and 1956, Seligmann was part of a group of young architects (including Bernhard Hoesli, Colin Rowe, John Hejduk, Robert Slutzky, Lee Hodgden and John Shaw) at the University of Texas in Austin, which set out to restructure architectural curricula. The group, which became known as the 'Texas Rangers', emphasized space, embraced history with the use of precedent, and included urban regionalism. This was radically different from the prevailing attitudes, which were devoid of history, regionalism and phenomenology. According to American architect Charles Moore, the programme at Texas stated that skill in architectural design involved three essential and interrelated abilities: to evolve an idea, to develop the idea in architectural terms, and to present the idea in drawings and models. We can see these being pursued by Rene in RT+Q and also in the studios he teaches at the Singapore University of Technology and Design.

Seligmann also wrote 'The Work of Le Corbusier as Lessons for the Student of Architecture' and managed to combine the ideas of Le Corbusier and Frank Lloyd Wright in his practice, as seen in his Barth David Synagogue. Similarly, we can glean from the operation of RT+Q the testing of ideas from the architects listed above and how they fit into the changing context. This brings us to Rene's encounter with Lerner and Ames, both of whom engaged in profound studies of geometry and composition in their projects. We can see a similar preoccupation for Rene in the paintings he worked on during the recent pandemic. The inability to travel physically led him to travel by imagining spaces and environments created out of compositions of geometries, volumes and colours. A musical aspect comes through in how the geometry and composition of the paintings sing, as Rene is after all a gifted musician, who can play pieces by Chopin on the grand piano during the middle of a conversation. The paintings give a hint, while listening to the piano

music, of how RT+Q's works manifest the adage that 'architecture is frozen music'.

When asked about other influences and points of reference, Rene lists:

Louis Kahn
    *Yale Center for British Art*
    *Kimbell Art Museum*
    *Salk Institute*
    *Esherick House*
    *Fisher House*

Wright
    *Prairie House*
    *Usonian Houses*

Le Corbusier
    *Pavillon Le Corbusier*

Jose Oubrerie
    *Miller House*

*The Rietveld Schröder House*

Comparing these references with the works of RT+Q, one can see them engaged in conversation. While creating something new today, the studio's projects are in dialogue with what came before and also with the works of tomorrow. It reflects a conviction that creativity is not just talent or originality, but more invention and synthesis. It is the ability to recognize, generalize and apply suitable architectural ideas to the problem at hand through the embrace of the history of architecture, both modern and pre-modern, which offers an enormous supply of forms and appearances as well as ideas and principles. This distinct and unique endeavour to view all architectural histories as vital sources of inspiration is nurtured and practised at RT+Q. Thus we see a willingness to openly acknowledge sources, to sieve through, to select, and to organize seemingly unrelated ideas into a constellation of useful and delightful environments. This forms a learning

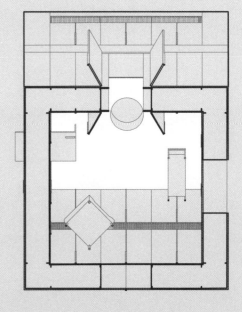

of architecture, a criticism of architecture and a celebration of architecture. It is what makes their architecture a sustainable practice and a legacy.

Besides Rene, there is another part of the equation 'RT + Q'. The 'Quality control' that its other partner, TK, brings, along with his deep knowledge and experience of administrative matters. He mentors the staff in realizing designs – the discipline to bring ideas to life by appreciating how things are built, knowing what regulations need to be observed and understanding the management of people involved in the creation and construction of these environments for many to enjoy. Without TK, wonderful and groundbreaking ideas may not see the light of day. Together with the presence of Jonathan, Sock Mui, Kai Li, Pek Hong and other members of the studio, they offer counterpoints to the melody that Rene plays to form a certain symphony that results in the RT+Q architecture.

And in this multiple, unique is RT+Q.

13

14    The bold looping form of the house is expressed in simple white plaster and paint.

# House at Holland

Rethinking tectonics with continuous form

Detached House, Singapore   2004–2006

The house opens to the better views at the front and rear.

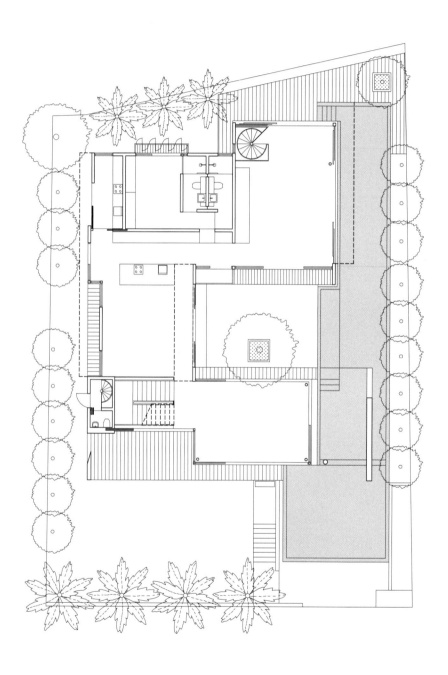

0   1   2        5m

An early project, this house proved seminal in our exploration of architecture not as decorative or applied art, but as plastic art. Without precedents, our search was intense, original and uninhibited. The probing of form was the foremost architectural intent – a result of Rene's recent return from the USA, where he had received the teachings of architects such as Michael Graves and the like. He led the office in reinterpreting the tropical dwelling via an abstracted, contemporary lexicon.

This house was built for a couple and their two sons. Floors, walls and ceilings are subsumed into a continuous band that loops and unfolds around the site so that the spaces within are encountered as a sequential 'gallery' of fluid and informal spaces. The C-shaped plan encloses a sunken courtyard on three sides, with the fourth side opening to the swimming pool. This void in the plan is an episode of visual and spatial calm amid the theatrics of the bold, sculpted mass.

The uneven topography of the slightly higher ground at the rear suggested a sectional approach to the design that combines high and intimate volumes. The entrance starts at the basement, which is level with the road. Garden steps lead to the ground-floor front garden, where an elevated deck perches like a stage and functions as ad-hoc seating for enjoying the garden. Behind the front façade, the three-storey staircase serves as a smaller sculpture within the larger sculpture of the building. Upward and downward, the residents' daily circulatory movements are constantly knitted to the external environment through glass walls. This is a counterintuitive moment in the programming, where a vehicle of utility becomes a prominent object of beauty.

The staircase joins the living room, whose step down in ceiling height is bluntly traced by the roof form. Here, we offered an alternative interpretation of the Urban Redevelopment Authority's attic guideline requiring a maximum pitch of 45 degrees. The standard response is a pitched roof, which if applied literally in this case would diminish our abstracted expressions. Our solution was to employ several mono-pitched roofs that emphasize the sense of movement accorded by the continuous structural band. While the design explores the relationship between the forms of the building, the weather and the natural landscape, it also examines the interaction between horizontal and vertical spaces. The former ensure ease of use and function, and the latter provides the drama.

Building materials were strategically deployed to aid the formal narrative. Plaster was used as a finishing material to sculpt, mould and articulate the forms; fair-faced concrete applied to elements such as the cantilevering carport accentuates the plasticity of the form and mass. Where there was the opportunity to express lightness of form and transparency, exposed steel and glass were used. The glass bridge connecting the public spaces upfront and private spaces in the rear is one such example.

The structure of the house has been designed to be expressive yet pragmatic. For example, the carport roof works as a privacy shield for the ground-floor spaces with its upward tilt. Counterintuitively, we capitalized on the raised profile to create a water feature, streaming water down the sloped profile into the swimming pool to add to the courtyard's sensorial abundance. In the ground-floor family room, a small spiral staircase offers alternative access to the basement study. Several features illuminate this space and acquaint it with adjacent spaces. One is a window cut into the swimming pool. Another is the bookshelf that visually connects the study and the family room above with a sliver of a skylight in the ground-floor slab.

Such details augment the experience of interior spaces as an interactive loop, which in turn reflects the continuous plastic form of the house itself.

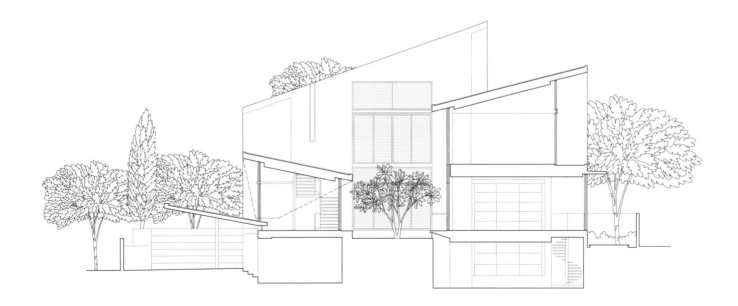

SECTION

0  1  2      5m

18    The staircase (top and right) forms part of the house's gallery of fluid spaces, while the swimming pool (bottom left) is an element of drama.

The sloped mono-pitch roof responds to attic guidelines in an abstract manner.

A glass bridge and large windows create an unhindered relationship between transitory zones and the courtyard.

The rear wing overlooking the courtyard houses the family room below and the master bedroom above.

Raising the living room from the ground level gives privacy and a vista of tree foliage.

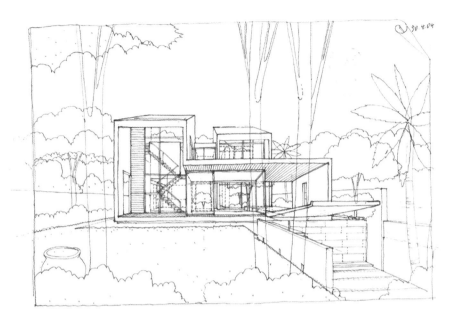

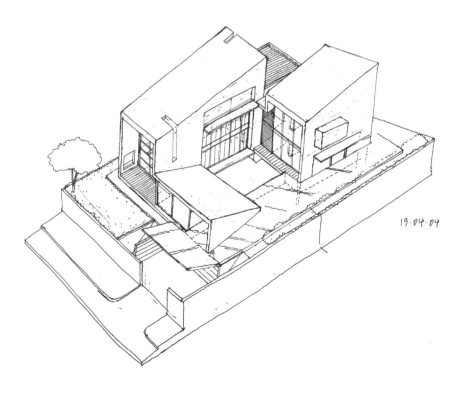

13.04.04

24   Slim pilotis express the first floor as a 'levitating' object (above); the pool as an extension of the guest bathroom (middle).

# House at Watten

The pursuit of plastic form in a terrace house

The courtyard view from the staircase.

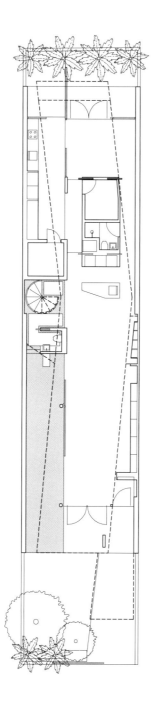

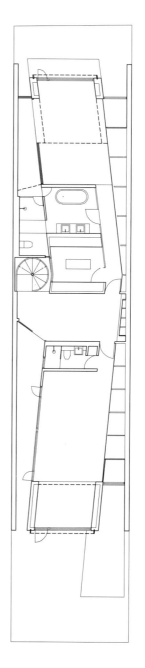

0 1 2          5m

Rene's move into a terraced house provided an opportunity early in our practice to dissect domestic tropes and find new expressions of tropical house design.

Our design bestows a sense of openness on the plot's narrow configuration, measuring approximately 6 x 35 metres (20 x 115 feet). It features the usual constraints of terraced homes – mainly a lack of light and ventilation. The challenge was to find a new, modern prototype for this typology, traditionally built up wall-to-wall; to re-examine the usual approach of terraced housing as 'infill' between the party walls; and to re-conceptualize the typical orthogonal air well design.

Our answer is a skewed form – akin to a boomerang or a banana – inserted between the party walls. Pried from the side walls and 'levitated' on slim piloti on the ground floor, the first-floor volume appears as a suspended object. Eschewing the usual domestic composition of planes and apertures, the house's expression becomes abstract. The residual voids at the side rising two-and-a-half storeys along the house's length are not only aesthetic but also functional. One of them houses a 2-metre-wide (6½-foot) lap pool that opens to the sky as a vehicle for light and air to penetrate the centre of the plan. It also doubles as an aquatic playground for

Rene's daughter. A storage space, wardrobe and bookshelves are carved into the other party wall to maximize space. The voids in between these elements channel natural light vertically between the ground- and first-floor spaces.

Despite its constrained setting, a layout that allows for fluid movement keeps the home feeling spatially unbounded. On the ground floor, the guestroom has double access, achieved by sacrificing a metre (3⅓ feet) of space for an additional corridor from the dry kitchen to the guestroom. These two openings allow unblocked views from the living room through the guestroom to the rear garden. To strengthen the reading of the house's monolithic form, it is finished entirely in a coat of white plaster and paint. This is complemented by nineteen other shades of white – in the furnishings, fittings, veneers, light oak laminate flooring, marble surfaces, and so on – that void the form of extraneous distractions of colour, materials or cladding. Instead of 'applied' detailing, the reinforced-concrete and steel house is abundant with construction detailing, such as grooves and gaps that demand precise workmanship.

Within the house, smaller sculptural components exhibit a formal virtuosity similar to that of the architecture. The compact spiral staircase, rendered in white plaster and paint, has curvaceous balustrades constructed of slim

timber panels that add to the house's language of lightness. It is accessed on the ground floor by stepping over a marble slab on a water body that turns the act of traversing up and down the house into a ritual. In the guest bathroom, the floating washbasin, expressed as an abstract cube, protrudes out of an aperture over the pool to bridge both internal and external areas.

House at Watten represents our firm belief that architecture must probe the realm of form. While the use of materials, clarity of structure and sophistication of detailing remain paramount, the preoccupation with clear and discernible form dominates. In line with our view of architecture as plastic art, the traditional representation of a house with a pitched roof and neat fenestrations is abolished in this project, thus creating architecture as a 'plastic event'.

At the same time, our discourse on form is not the only element behind the design. The house was devised to be sustainable in the way it minimizes resources and limits the strategic design decisions with purposeful, articulated parts. The architecture is simple, and built with basic materials and methods. Its elements extract from nature to perform – water for landscaping in the pool, natural light from the chasm for maximum illumination, light and air permeating from the voids in the house's distorted form.

SECTION

0  1  2          5m

A spiral staircase compacts the vertical access into an elegant sculpture (above); the language of geometric precision at the courtyard (top and bottom).

Bands of grey granite frame the courtyard (top); the naturally illuminated master bathroom (bottom); the guest bathroom basin's cubic expression at the pool (above).

# Double 'C' House
Reframing the architectural shell

Extended roof eaves and overlapping forms create semi-sheltered tropical spaces.

Set amid mature foliage in its north and east elevations, with a canal to the south, this plot enjoys pleasant views and a rare seclusion akin to being in a tropical resort. Instinctively, we turned the vistas of our design inward towards these green views. The main massing comprises two C-shaped concrete shells, whose stretched eaves provide shelter for the internal spaces. They face each other across a 24-metre (79-foot) swimming pool, with the symmetry and strong axial organization taking a page from classical architecture. The void between the C-shaped volumes works like a courtyard to detach spaces physically but link them visually. At the front of the plot, the carport canopy is clad with timber to distinguish it from the main house while connecting it to its natural context.

The footprint of the two-storey house dominates the site, but the scale is controlled. The intent was to create a union of building and nature through tall and open volumes, voids in the architecture and sheltered, semi-open spaces such as terraces. As the land slopes higher to the north, the bedrooms and communal spaces were raised to the first floor, while less light-sensitive rooms such as utility spaces, an art gallery and storage spaces were positioned on the semi-sunken ground floor. The C-shaped blocks give order to the spatial organization: one contains the living room, and the other houses a guestroom and the master bedroom. A 'bridge' volume containing the kitchen and dining room connects them across the swimming pool.

The entrance sequence starts by traversing a stone platform that is flanked by pools of water. Opacity versus transparency, heaviness versus lightness, movement versus stillness – the many

The arrival sequence leads from the foyer on lower ground to an event of light and greenery above.

contradictions within this small space create a deeply sensorial prelude. A black stone-clad wall terminates the end of the space. It stops short of meeting the ceiling, leaving a sliver of glass that illuminates the foyer and frames the crown of trees in the distance. This gap is also our attempt to differentiate the upper and lower volumes so that the dining room reads as a box floating on the water. A transparent wall on one side of the foyer signals the formal entrance, into which we embedded the front door, composed of timber screens. Beyond it, a staircase framed in steel and with floating treads presents itself as a sculptural object detached from the wall.

Extruded along the length of the site, the C-shaped forms perpetuate a longitudinal encounter with the landscape. Nature is experienced in a series of slow reveals that culminate in a thick wall of greenery next to the terrace of the master bedroom. A row of sliding timber screens fronts the northern block, buffering the corridor outside the bedrooms. Like morphing skins, they give the elevation different expressions depending on the owners' needs. The screens are distributed throughout the building where necessary for privacy and sun control, and as a motif to soften the brutalist shell.

Robust and simple, the material palette contributes to the creation of tranquil spaces. Off-form concrete, stone, glass and timber are employed in ways to clearly express planes and volumes, and the integration of stainless steel into details articulates edges and frames elements. In the master bedroom, the canvas of white paint and marble acts as a foil to the greenery, which is framed through slot windows and a centrally located skylight. The rooms are generously sized and rectilinear in plan to allow the owners to adapt the spaces with their personal touch and give longevity to the architecture. In 2021, they sold the house to new owners, who have engaged us to help renovate it for a different demographic and lifestyle. It presents an exciting opportunity to revisit one of our older works for the very first time.

SECTION

0  1  2      5m

Timber screens filter light and views in the corridor outside the master bedroom.

The white surfaces of the master bathroom contrast with the brutalist shell.

The lower-ground entrance foyer is naturally lit by a gap between the dining-room slab and the swimming pool.

The main spaces were designed without false ceilings for purity of material and form.

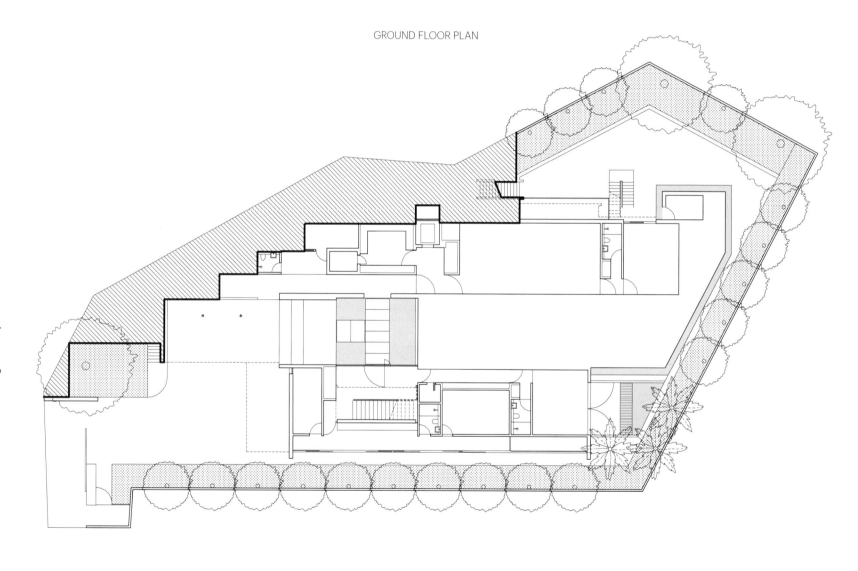

0   2    5           10m

FIRST FLOOR PLAN

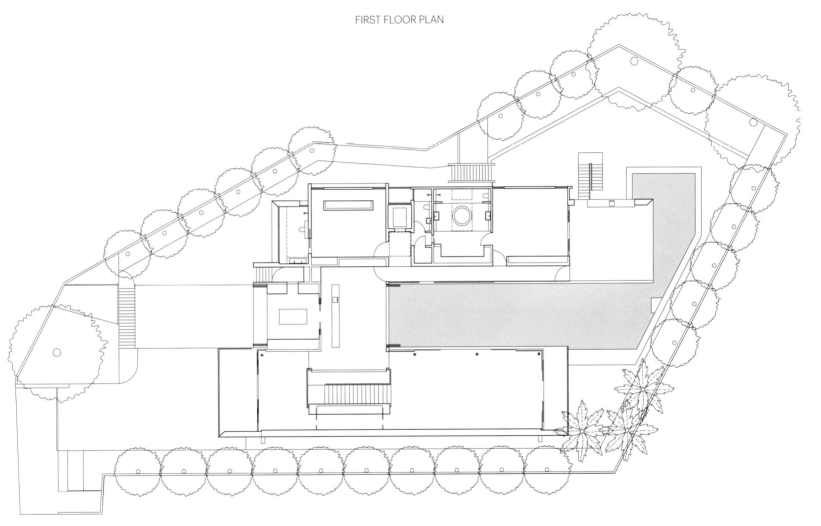

The two-block massing clearly defines public and private spaces, linked by the dining room.

# House at Damansara

Rethinking relationships of enclosure and form

An open, grand space defines one side of the 'spine' (above and opposite top), while the other side is private and intimate (opposite bottom).

Two lines with a box on each side – one open, the other enclosed. This parti (key concept diagram) of the House at Damansara is an exercise in brevity. The client had acquired the elevated land behind his tropical-style house and was eager to build a 650-square-metre (7,000-square-foot) annex in a different architectural language. It was to expand the living and entertainment spaces, both externally and internally, with more gardens, a new lap pool, a second kitchen and a larger master bedroom en suite.

Our response is a paean to the modernist canon, appropriated to the tropical setting. It is an exploration of tropical architecture in the most minimal and abstract manner, enabled through a considered combination of materials and logical, rigorous detailing. Like our earlier works House at Holland and House at Watten (see pp. 14 and 24), this house continues pushing the boundaries of architecture as plastic art, albeit using more simplified expressions. Our intention to have the new house contrast with yet respect the original residence resulted in a clear and elemental foil to the latter.

The interplay of lines and planes, horizontals and verticals is employed as visual and spatial tools to navigate the site and spaces. Two parallel walls bisect the rectangular plot as the main organizing component, stretching up two storeys to claim an assertive presence on the site. They form a corridor that delineates private from public spaces, while openings on their lawn-facing surfaces mitigate the wall's monumentality and offer views.

In our reinterpretation of the tropical house, the living room presents itself as an abstracted pavilion set in a garden. It is detached visually from the spine with slivers of glass as a 7-metre-tall (23-foot) cube – providing drama with its sheer scale and pure form. Full-height, powder-coated sliding windows on two facing elevations are set in to shelter the interiors like the vernacular tropical house. They frame views of the existing house towards the rear and the vast lawn upfront. While both houses read as distinct entities, they are connected by the sharing of courtyard views from their kitchens, with the new overlooking the old from higher ground.

Designed to accommodate garden parties, the lawn is edged with stainless-steel plates that give the illusion of a floating plane of green – a gesture left intact from the eventually abandoned intention for a basement car park. Another steel plate sharpens the edge of the living room's external profile, adding definition and depth while reflecting our belief in the importance of the artful termination of edges. The palette for the rest of the house is equally modest but purposeful. Plaster and paint dominate, but off-form concrete and black granite cladding combine to present an impenetrable front to the road. This gives way to a porous interior with panels of timber brise-soleil neatly integrated into the blockish composition, naturally ventilating and giving privacy to many parts of the home.

Very rarely does a project show consistency from ideation to construction, but we managed to achieve it here because of the outstanding builders who observed, laboured over and cared for every detail. The client also seized every opportunity that we visited Kuala Lumpur for another project to check on the house's progress – and was completely on board with us in experimenting with a new approach to architecture and lifestyle.

GROUND FLOOR PLAN

FIRST FLOOR PLAN

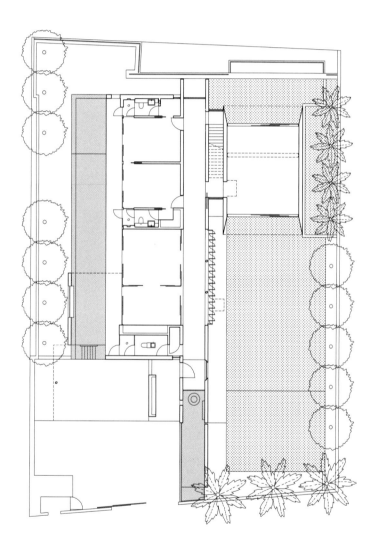

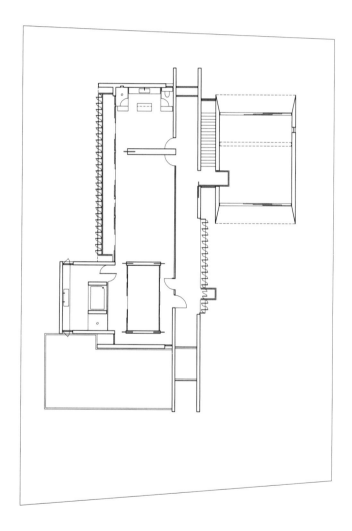

0    2    5            10m

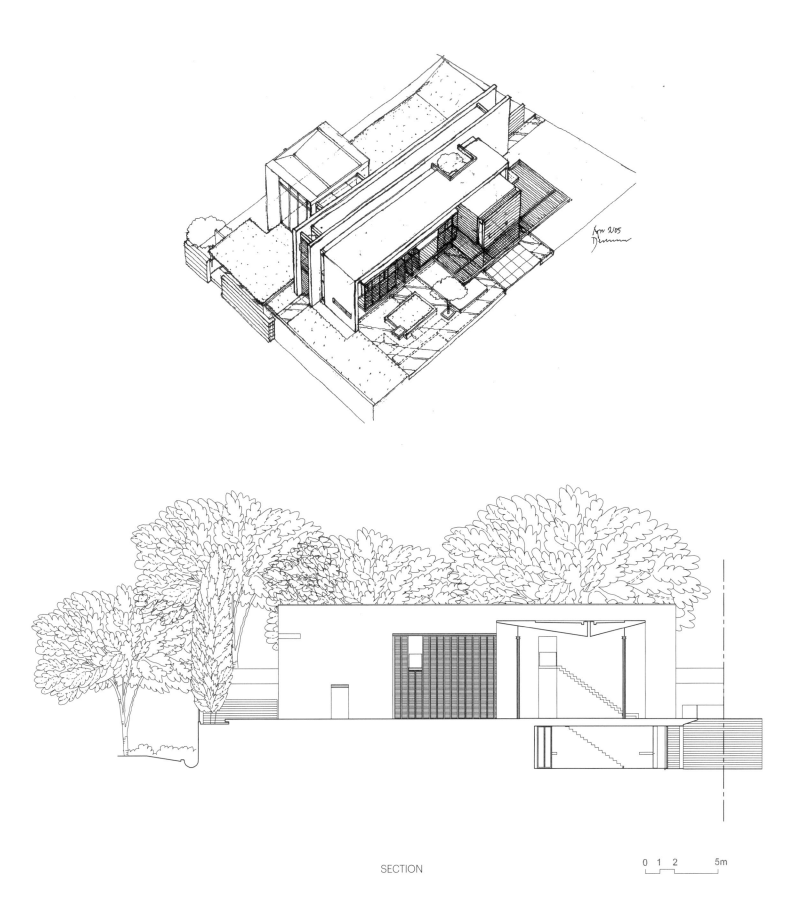

SECTION

0 1 2     5m

The living-room block's transparency links it with the old house at the rear.

Cut-outs in the large planes lend surprise to the composition.

48    Pivoting screens buffer the bedrooms from neighbours (above), while Juliet balconies connect spaces (middle).

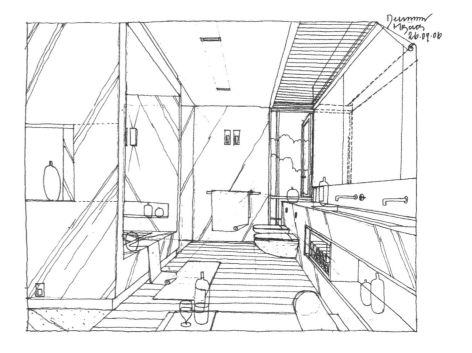

The bathtub in the master bathroom was conceived as an entity within a larger space.

The arrangement of volumes around the pool creates an external courtyard.

# House at Cable

An unexpected dialogue between old and new

Conserved Detached House, Singapore    2007–2009

The asymmetrical architecture of the old house is mediated by the symmetry of the new interventions.

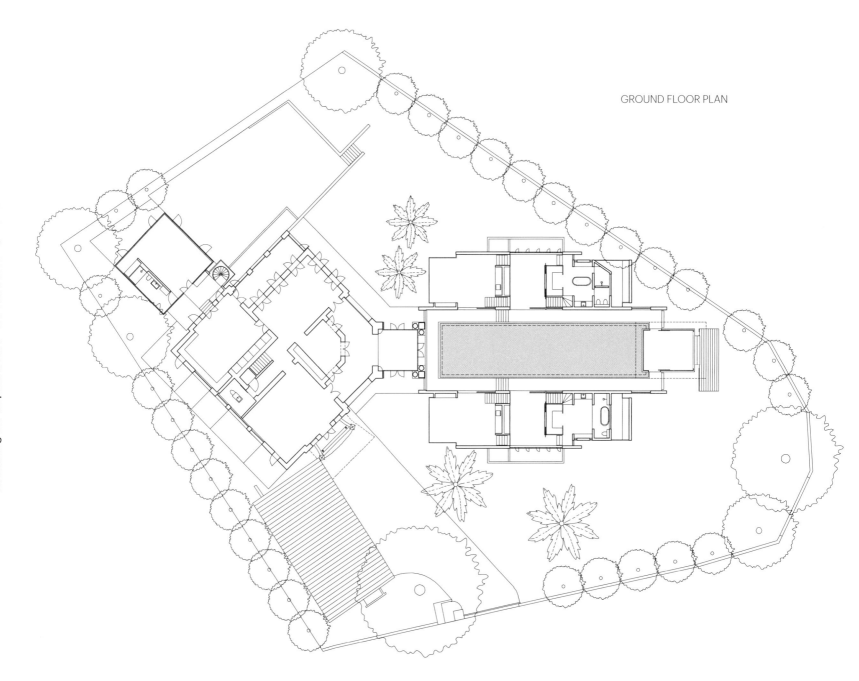

GROUND FLOOR PLAN

0    2    5        10m

One of the few restoration and adaptive reuse projects we have been fortunate to work on is this conserved black and white detached house. It is challenging to mediate with existing parameters compared to new builds but we are pushed into deeper negotiations and discussions on context and dwelling. While the client had a simple brief to add more space to the existing house for two grown children, guests, back-of-house facilities and a carport for five cars, it was complicated by the local authority's strict conservation guidelines.

Such houses were built for wealthy European immigrants sent to Singapore during the British Empire in the 19th and early 20th centuries. This particular structure was designed by British architect David McLeod Craik of Swan & Maclaren in 1913 for the municipal councillor Mohamed Ali Namazi. While it is not colossal by the standards of the time, its formal elements give it a monumental presence. The charming edifice is detailed in the then-popular Tropical Edwardian style, where beams, walls and fenestrations were distinguished in trademark monochromatic paint. Components drawn from vernacular architecture were incorporated for harmonious living in the tropical climate before air-conditioning was invented. Flooring – tiles on the ground floor and timber on the first – was chosen for the ability to provide coolness underfoot, while long eaves and balconies buffer rooms from rainfall, heat and glare.

Unlike the Palladian style commonly adopted by black and white detached houses of the early 20th century, whose layout follows the classical dictates of a central axis, this house has a diamond-shaped plan, with the front porch set in one corner at a 45-degree angle to the main body. This positioning aligns the front of the house towards the longest length of the leafy corner plot, giving the windows on this façade a long garden vista. Deciding where to place the extensions presented a dilemma, as conservation guidelines would not allow any new buildings at the front of the house in order to respect the historical house's visage. However, the sides and rear were cramped. We managed to tuck the carport and guest wings to the sides, and after considering several iterations, decided to go ahead with the somewhat irreverent strategy of placing the son's and daughter's quarters in front of the main entrance. It was finally approved on the condition that they remain at one-storey height.

Two modern, identical long blocks extend from the existing house, leaving plenty of garden space around. Abstract and solid, they are quiet foils to the conserved building's intricacies and cultural nuances. The discreet palette of white paint, grey granite and marble pays homage to the existing building's simple plaster-and-paint attributes. The volumes are dematerialized at the front edge with glass, lightening their mass in deference to the older structure.

The swimming pool was placed between the two blocks, where it becomes a meeting place for the family akin to the forum in Roman architecture. A small gym block is the fourth edge of this courtyard. Enclosed in glass, it frames a clear view of the existing building. Our architectural strategy clearly delineates old from new, but also knits the former into a new relationship with the site. Our interventions, while contemporary, are still grounded in classical principles of symmetry, hierarchy and proportion, reiterated by bands of timber screens facing the pool. The path around the water body takes one through sequences of openness and enclosure – a plan inspired by the Villa of the Papyri, a grand Roman courtyard house in Herculaneum, Italy, which was buried under volcanic ash when Vesuvius erupted in 79 CE.

For the existing house, the goal was to preserve its spirit as much as possible. The dilapidated structure was meticulously restored as a venerable object. Damaged parts were reconstructed referencing old photographs and the staircase was rebuilt. The balustrades, ornamental timber lattices, timber shutters, French windows, timber floors and patterned floor tiles were cleaned up and reinstated, along with the classical details of the exterior architraves and columns. On the first floor, the balconies are layered with frameless glass as the owners prefer air-conditioned spaces. A pleasant sunroom results at the front veranda. The porch on the ground floor, also encased in frameless glass, morphs from an end point into a threshold, mitigating the two generations of structures inside the house. We exposed the elaborate timber structure to exhibit the sensible architecture, which optimizes airflow by drawing hot air upward and out while providing daylight at the heart of the diamond-shaped plan.

This project addresses the attributes of a sustainable built environment in various ways. The strategy of adaptive reuse enhances the idea of longevity and its noteworthiness. The house has been conserved to retain memories, and altered to accommodate new needs and lifestyles. It endures by responding to change. Our unorthodox resolution between the old and new volumes exhibits a rethinking of the traditional programming of space. What was once a sole building becomes almost like a series of pavilions with extended experiences to nature, water, wind and light. While this new arrangement stirred some controversy, it also resulted in invaluable discourse on conservation. In 2011, it earned an Architectural Heritage Award from Singapore's Urban Redevelopment Authority, proving that relevance and respect need not be mutually exclusive.

The restored lantern roof (above left); and the house before restoration (above right).

The new blocks are read as separate yet integrated with the existing form.

A sunroom extends from the master bedroom (top); the dining room (bottom left); and the walkway to the living room (bottom right).

The existing house's front porch becomes a gateway to the extensions.

SECTION

0   2   5   10m

The new blocks are a tempered composition of screens, glass and paint, with granite cladding the bathrooms (this page).

The new sightlines create a strong relationship between old and new.

# House at Pondok Indah

Tropicalizing the Prairie-style house

The simplicity of the architecture is enhanced by the considered termination of edges and corners.

The low-hipped roofs with extended eaves give a tropicality to the simple modernist box.

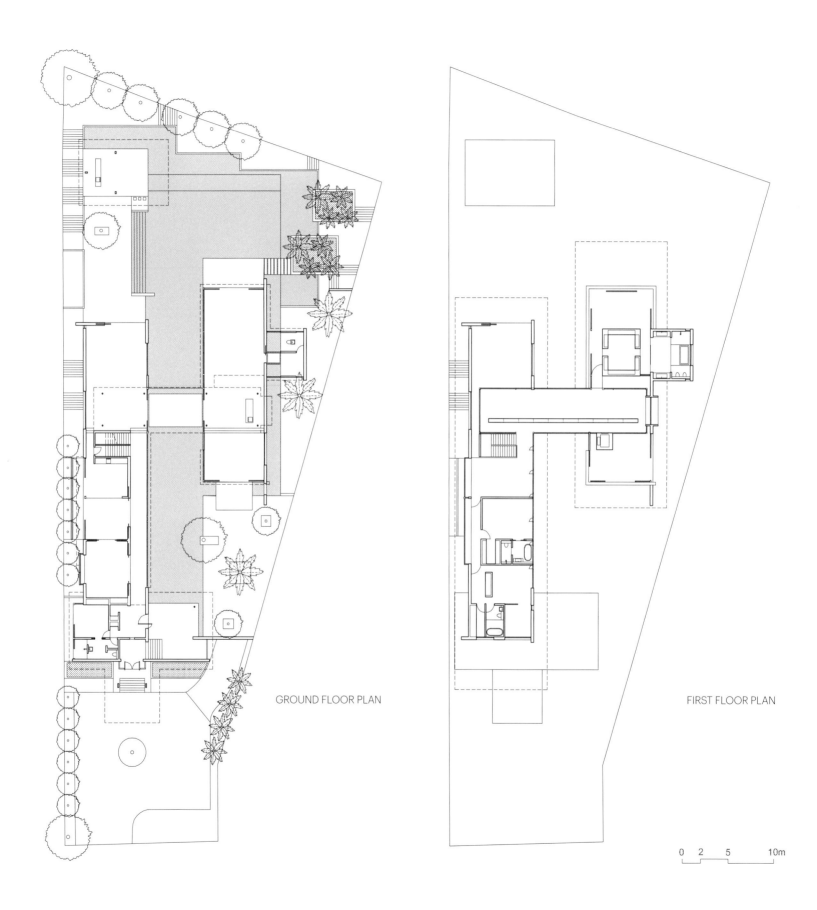

GROUND FLOOR PLAN

FIRST FLOOR PLAN

0    2    5        10m

Located in an upscale residential neighbourhood in the region of Kebayoran Lama, South Jakarta, this house is pivotal in our oeuvre. It freed us from the shackles of an abstract modernist approach embodied in the purist cube form to explore the regional vernacular archetype's distinct expressions of roof and walls. We owe this to the house's enlightened owner, who studied architecture (though he never practised). He admired the work of humanist architect Frank Lloyd Wright, particularly the Robie House from his Prairie-style series, with its iconic horizontal rooflines, far-reaching eaves and open plan, which inspired the formal direction of this house.

As always, the attempt was to design with as few formalistic moves as possible. The concept is essentially a two-storey house with pronounced roofs. The massing is simple, comprising three long bands laid out as two parallel blocks and a connecting, smaller glass bridge. They are all knitted together by gardens and water. A central pond segues into a swimming pool, with an infinity edge that leads the eye forward into the green expanse of a golf course at the site's rear. The water elements both calm and stir the senses with moving reflections of light and shadow upon white ceilings. Tucking the car park for six cars in the basement freed up space on the ground floor for these phenomenological episodes.

The plan mirrors the plot – shaped like a fan, with the more intimate width at the entrance. Rejecting convention, we placed the more public areas such as the living room and dining room at the farther end of the trajectory from the main door to allow this space a full prospect of the borrowed greenery. The transparency of the architecture through full-height glass walls and windows brings picturesque vistas inward. Five-metre (16-foot) roof overhangs and aluminium sun-shading fins moderate the severe heat and glare of the tropics, even with the generous use of glass.

To display the client's impressive art collection, the glass bridge takes on a second role as an art gallery, with its capacious width giving it the attribute of a room rather than a passageway. It connects bedrooms in one wing to the master bedroom en suite in the other wing. The simplicity of the architecture demanded a high level of detailing, which comes through in the exposed steel structure, the concise aluminium screens and the pronounced profile of roof edges. The privacy and sun-shading screens envelop the master bedroom to give it a horizontal emphasis that contrasts with the verticality of the adjacent block containing the double-storey dining room. Their uncomplicated materials serve as a foil for the richness of travertine, Statuario marble, Makassar ebony wood and mosaic tiles, composed in clear blocks and planes to confer a sense of dignity to form, space and thresholds.

While Wright's houses were the inspiration for this dwelling's expressions, the architecture is a response to the pre-existing set of conditions. It addresses the attributes of a sustainable built environment in various ways, particularly a harmony with place. Its design participates in and symphonizes with the suburban character of the Jakarta neighbourhood but with self-definition and confidence. Pitched roofs, brise-soleil and local materials form the visual vocabulary of the architecture, resulting in a house that merges with the history and culture of the place. Such a discussion has continued in our subsequent projects, including the House with a Roof (pp. 218–227).

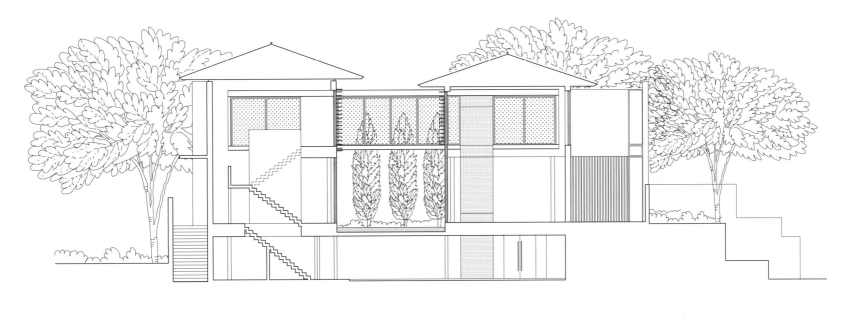

SECTION

0  1  2          5m

The living room enjoys expansive views of the lush golf course at its back door.

The glass bridge lightens the house's architectonics.

The house's many water elements provide a sensorial counterpoint to the strict tectonics.

The gallery-cum-bridge is expressed as both an internal and an external volume.

The ensemble of forms is designed to frame the landscape.

# House in Three Movements

A three-part harmony of form, material and light

The house is offset from the boundary walls to read as an autonomous volume.

The 8-metre-high (26-foot) blocks are separated by 2-metre-wide (6½-foot) voids.

GROUND FLOOR PLAN

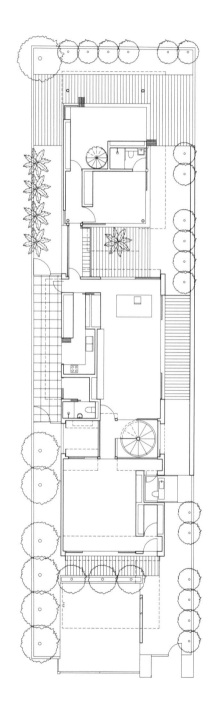

FIRST FLOOR PLAN

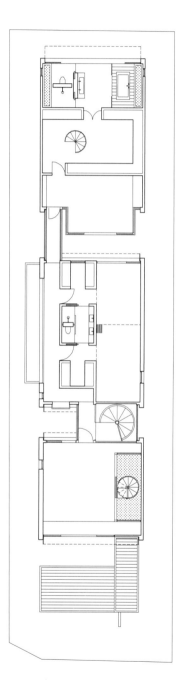

0  1  2        5m

Is a house that claims every square metre of land a better house? Must a house confine itself to the aesthetic of a single volume to feel cohesive? How can modulating the standard idea of a house affect the interior experience? This house rethinks the suburban single-family dwelling by challenging conventions of massing as well as spatial organization and relationships in the residential typology.

The original semi-detached house's adjoining twin had been redeveloped into a detached structure. Our first point of irreverence was to mirror this by setting the house back 2 metres (6½ feet) from the party wall. The narrowing of the house on an already limited 11-metre-wide (36-foot) plot increased the demands on the design. We then segmented the house into three 8-metre-high (26-foot) cubes strung along the deep plot. This formal proposition is rooted in musical form, where the organization of a sonata or symphony, each comprising several varied movements that fuse into a unified composition, informs the massing and tempo of the architecture.

Just as these movements accord a sense of proportion and scale to a long piece of music, so the datum – in this case, the repetitive octagonal volumes – sections the house into more intimate portions. It corresponds with the client's request for a 'layering of building blocks', each housing distinct functions. We differentiated the cladding for each volume – timber strips, white plaster and paint, and striated textured concrete – to distinguish the character of each 'movement'.

Courtyards and glass bridges heighten the separation of the volumes as much as they connect them. They weave intermittent episodes of light and verdant vistas into the house's trajectory, much like the way in which air wells in the shophouse vernacular (see p. 125) bring relief to a deep plan. The massing effectively results in three little houses within the plan, each with light and views on all four sides. This increases the four elevations of a conventional dwelling to six. The augmented transparency extends the line of sight through the home and intensifies the light to imbue the interiors with a sense of spaciousness. The exposure to greenery as one traverses from one cube to another intensifies the sense of time and place.

The intention was to express each of the different functions in a separate block – the main public areas in one, the daughters in their own little 'house', and the owners' retreat in a third. Progressing from public to private, the first volume stacks the music room on top of the living room, the second houses the kitchen and dining with the two daughters' bedrooms above and the audio-visual room and maids' quarters in the basement. The innermost volume is a sanctum containing the guestroom and study below and the master bedroom above. We echoed the house's three-part form with three spiral staircases, one installed in each volume. These sculptural features are a leitmotif in creating a coherent architecture, and also heighten the house's sectional character. The largest staircase tunnels from the basement to the first floor between the first two blocks. The second winds up from the study to the master wardrobe, and the third is a lithe contraption pictured against a green wall leading to a roof terrace, with the view of the park across the road.

While what is most overt about the house is the arrangement of its massing, the interstitial spaces defining the beginnings and ends of each volume are what enrich the internal experiences. These thresholds are detailed with great care to address space and edge. For example, a U-shaped timber fin lines the first block's façade like eyelashes, filtering sunlight, softening hard lines, mitigating scale and enlivening the architecture. This may not be one of the largest projects in our oeuvre, but its parti (key concept diagram) is one of the clearest and its form one of the most abstract.

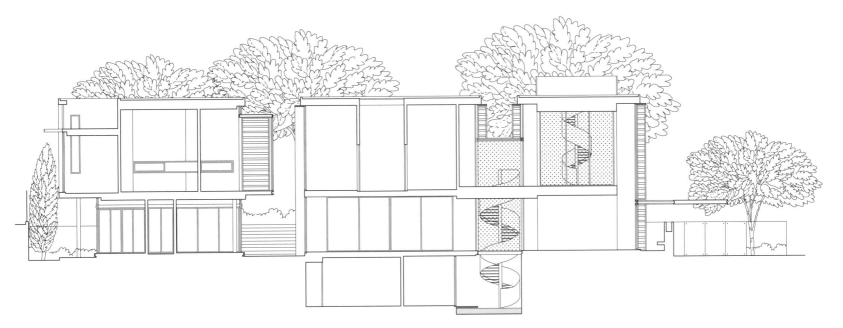

SECTION

0  1  2        5m

74    The circular geometry of vertical accesses, including the spiral staircase, forms a secondary narrative (above and opposite).

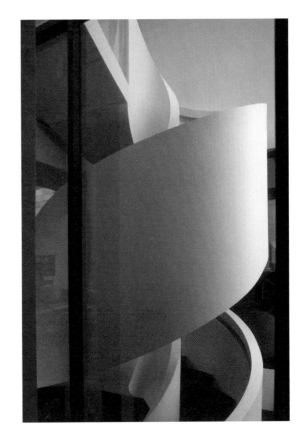

Sliding glass doors rising to 7.5 metres (24½ feet) accentuate the living room's partial double-height space.

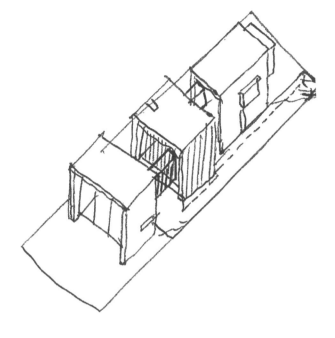

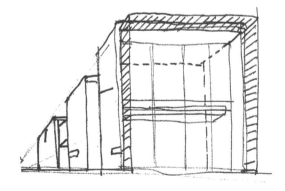

A lithe spiral staircase gracefully connects the piano room to the rooftop.

The surface of the reflective pool appears to merge with the swimming pool and the sea beyond.

# Shorefront

A counterintuitive approach to seaside residences

Condominium, Penang, Malaysia   2006–2018

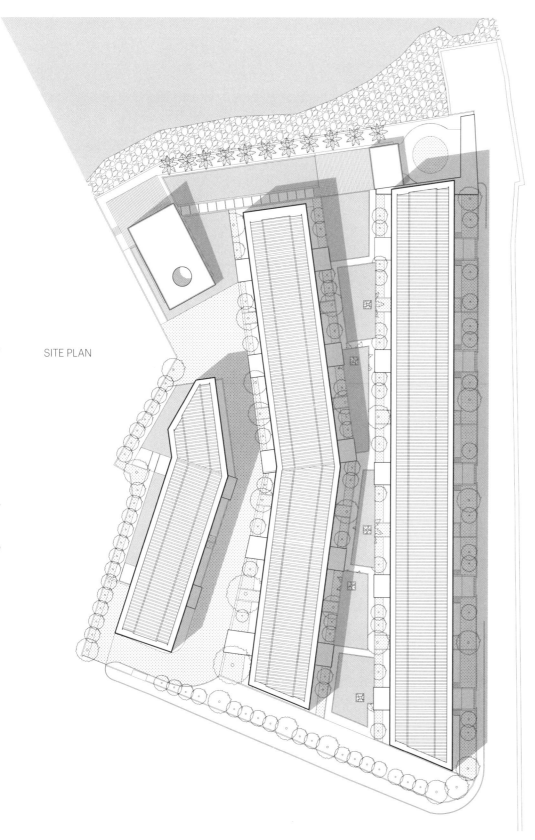

SITE PLAN

This condominium development is located in the buffer zone of the historic area of George Town, Penang, which has been recognized as a UNESCO World Heritage Site since 2008. The town's rich history as the first British settlement in Southeast Asia and a once-thriving entrepôt is reflected in the numerous historical buildings surrounding the rectilinear site. One of these is the grand Eastern & Oriental Hotel built by the Sarkies Brothers in 1885, which is a direct neighbour along one long edge of the plot. The site's other long edge borders a field that buffers it from two prestigious schools, one of which was founded in the 19th century. The two short ends present opposing characteristics: one faces the busy Lebuh Farquhar (Farquhar Street), a major thoroughfare that has existed since the 18th century, while the other opens to picturesque views of the sea that surrounds Penang Island.

The architectural resolution is thus a highly contextual response to this variety of situations. Rather than creating a self-glorifying edifice, we worked towards an amicable balance of scale, sense of place and restrained luxury for this over 100-unit estate. George Town-based SM OOI Architect was the local architecture firm.

This plot is a unique seafront site in the historic locale, giving it eminence and exclusivity.

It was thus natural that the client requested that every unit have a sea view. This would have been impossible if we had settled for a massing that paralleled the edge of the sea, as this frontage lies at one of the short ends of the site. Instead, we conceived three long blocks that trace the plot's length inward, which achieves for each unit oblique vistas of the tranquil waters through the voids between each block. This massing also produces other advantages: sea breezes pass through the voids to gift each unit with good airflow, and the residents enjoy city views in the other direction, anchoring them to their urban context.

The plot's location in a sensitive part of town meant that it came with severe building restrictions, such as stringent setbacks from the water and the road, and a height control. Each block in the low-density development was capped at five storeys, comprising two duplexes stacked atop single-storey ground-floor units with gardens. We gave the top units open roof terraces, sheltered with trellises, as privileged areas for enjoying the sun and sights.

The functional brief was straightforward, but we sought to reimagine the human-centric qualities of living in the dense city. The layout of the adjacent duplex units is alternated from front to rear such that no unit's glassed front elevation faces another unit's front, enabling the balconies to be enjoyed privately. For added privacy, we covered the rear of each unit with screens. Brise-soleil shielding the private lift lobbies adds to this matrix of glass and screens on the façade that reduces the perceived bulk of the long blocks. A quintessentially modern language emerges, yet it is not jarring to its surroundings. The one-unit-deep plans further accentuate the porous architecture.

The duplex units facing the sea are the most luxurious. They are designed to be as open as possible to unite the interiors with the water. In contrast, the units that bookend the street have controlled views through smaller apertures. While the blocks help establish the development's relationship to the neighbourhood, the voids between the blocks are treated with equal importance, being designed as serene urban respites for the residents. One void features a grassy lawn. In the other, we stitched a series of shallow pools into a water garden that offers ambling residents a meditative stroll. The pools inject a sense of formality into the space but also serve as a subtle means of deterring noisy loiterers outside the homes.

These negative spaces were designed after the sublime courtyard of Louis Kahn's Salk Institute in La Jolla, California, which extends infinity sightlines out to the sea and formulates a meditative atmosphere. Like this precedent, nothing in the development disturbs the serenity of the horizon line at the seafront end – except for a slight, playful gesture that marries landscape, urban sculpture and architecture. The roof of the gym's courtyard is subtly lifted to call attention to a circular skylight that brings light into the sunken space. From inside, attention is drawn skyward in another meditative act.

The forms on-site are linked to the context of sea and city.

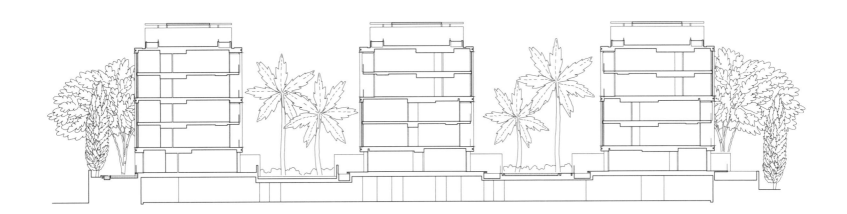

SECTION

0    5    10    15m

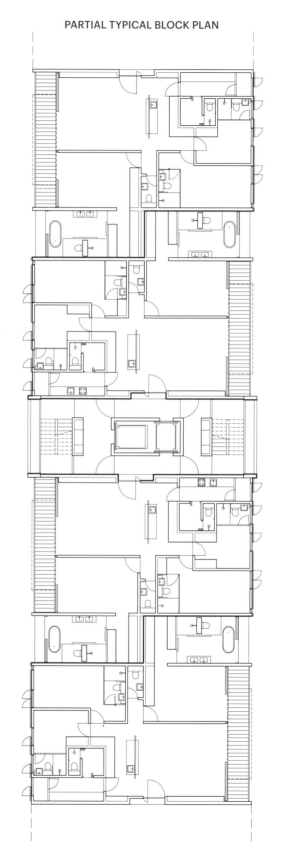

The public spaces are designed with a unique sense of space, such as the ponds between the blocks (top).

0  1  2        5m

The sunken gym's courtyard, with its circular skylight (opposite bottom and above).

84    The composition expresses a stacking of two double-storey units above one-storey units on the ground floor.

Guest bathrooms (top) and double-height balconies (bottom) take advantage of the panoramic views.

Subtle details articulate the edge of the building.

# Sentul East

Detailing a new tropical model for working and living

The industrial materiality and irregular form of The Capers are a counterpoint to the standard architectural language of surrounding buildings.

Details of metallic fins and edges preserve the architecture's proportions and geometry.

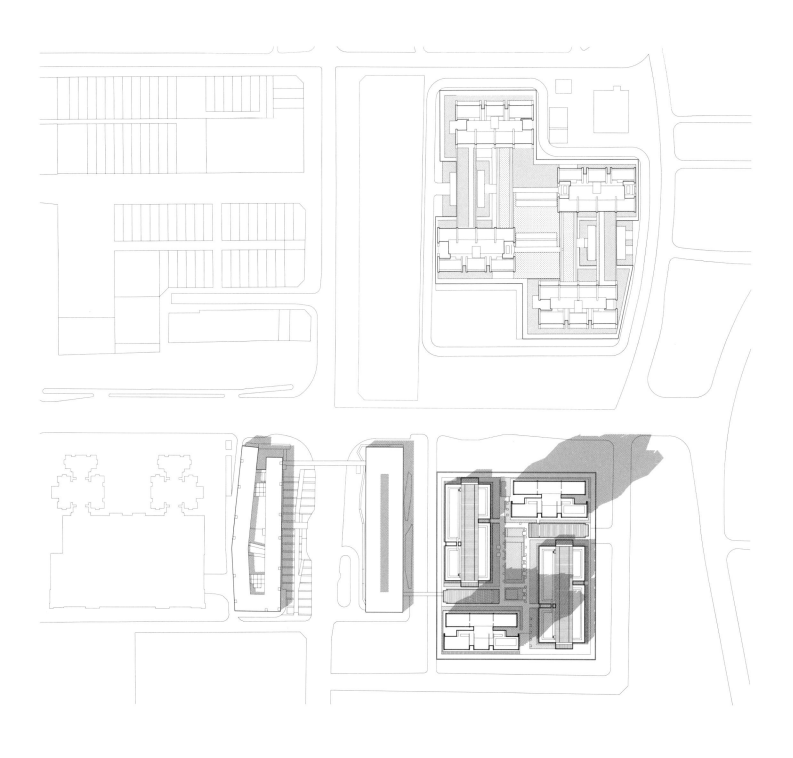

SITE PLAN

0    20    50    100m

The collection of three projects is part of the reinvigoration of the Sentul township, a city backwater some 5 kilometres (3 miles) north of Kuala Lumpur. Once a flourishing railway depot, the area slid into decline after the Second World War until the intervention of our client, a well-established Malaysian developer. They conceived of a 44-hectare (108-acre) urban renewal project known as the Sentul Masterplan to rejuvenate the hodgepodge sprawl of historic colonial detached houses, nondescript low-rise shops, revered religious buildings and large warehouses left over from the former railway industry.

By the time we joined the project, three other residential towers in the masterplan had already been realized by other architects. Our contribution to residential, commercial, retail and urban design was guided by two simple aims. One was to create landmarks and a sense of urban order within the hybridized cityscape. The other was to lay the groundwork for livable and inspiring spaces for the people who inhabit and use them.

## d7 and d6

These two office blocks located in the designated live-work-play zone of Sentul East are low-rise and distinctively modern buildings. They greet each other from across the busy thoroughfare of Jalan Sentul and are linked by a bridge, creating a gateway into the development. We questioned the formulaic template of the traditional office block with an architecture that put workers' wellbeing at the fore. The porosity of the ground level on both blocks invites public participation with food and beverage as well as retail components. They also take advantage of the tropical conditions, with the introduction of green elements on the ground level that result in lively and inviting respites for both pedestrians and office workers.

Like siblings, the two blocks share similar window designs but embody opposing expressions of darkness and light, mass and skin. d7 is a solid seven-storey volume clad in aluminium panels. The bold, simple and somewhat severe façade offers a confident presence amid the urban squalor. Windows shaped like Tetris blocks give the façade a sense of scale. The varied L-shaped openings also reflect the multiple office configurations on offer, some with double-volume spaces. As d7 is sited on a larger plot, we were able to carve out a generous internal courtyard on the ground floor. The building's form cranks outward at the rear as if pushed out by this void, thus turning a ubiquitous box into sculpture. This gesture is a display and affirmation of our belief in architecture as a plastic art with malleable form, as well as a rethinking of the office building typology.

Although sacrificing a large piece of land for the courtyard runs counter to the dogma in office real estate to maximize rentable space, it is imperative in our design. The courtyard is the soul of the building, an informal space for gathering and spontaneous exchange akin to an 'agora' or 'intellectual forum'. This is accentuated by dark granite slabs, timber platforms, seating, ponds and creepers strung on stainless-steel cables that ascend seven storeys up the void – all coming together to offer a moment of escape from the daily grind. In addition, shade, greenery, breezes and speckled sunshine make it a pleasant and thermally inviting space, while glass bridges at different levels of the building accentuate connectivity and conviviality.

In contrast, d6 is an architecture of light, skin and depth. The six-storey massing is distinguished by an outer membrane of expanded metal mesh that catches the light like gossamer to bring about dynamism in the façade. This language of transparency and translucency adds complexity to the simple box form while functioning as an environmental shield. On its eastern façade, a mesh skin invites planters and creepers to coexist with the architecture. A spine of skylights punctures the roof, an architectural illuminator that brings sunlight deep into the plan. Garden suites on the second floor offer visual relief and surprise, while on the ground floor, a water garden at the rear rendered as reflective shards is a quiet and meditative urban marker.

The designs of d6 and d7 reflect an aim to redefine the workplace and a belief in how a biophilic environment can help alleviate the pressures of work. The blocks also weave into Jalan Sentul's envisioned future as a lushly landscaped boulevard linking subsequent components of the development. By creating their own context in an environment without one, the animated windows and green features of both blocks actively pursue a dialogue between the street and the architecture, and inject a sense of warmth into a conventionally sombre archetype.

## The Capers

This condominium tested our approach to counterintuitive thinking of house design in the context of residential high-rise typology. Occupying a 1.7-hectare (4.3-acre) land parcel within the larger Sentul Masterplan, it features a pair of thirty-six-storey blocks and two five-storey townhouse blocks rising from the piano nobile of a landscaped car park podium. We envisioned creating a new urban environment to stimulate urban revival and provide 500 units of mid-cost housing comprising flats, maisonettes, penthouses, bridge units and townhouses. They are designed around a 'forum' of landscaping, greenery, water features, swimming pools, pavilions and amenities such as function rooms, gymnasiums, prayer rooms, childcare centres, playgrounds and laundromats – essentially a vital microcosm of a larger, mature urban context.

Our two zig-zag building forms eschewed the safe yet colourless standard straight block. They have since become endearing visual markers in the neighbourhood, garnering such nicknames as 'the crooked, or *bengkok*, building', 'the up-ended battleship' and 'the kris' (a curvy blade with Indonesian origins) among taxi drivers and curious onlookers. The search for architectural form began with an interpretation of the site on our first visit: a flat, barren terrain of wild grass, grazing cows and reeds among a rugged landscape of greenery and parks. The organic forms of the towers draw inspiration from the soft, billowing local lalang (coarse grass) that grew wild in the area. A second inspiration was an urban icon: the elementary and commonplace jagged yellow road marking. Inspiration, we believe, can originate from the most unlikely sources. The Capers is a 'relative' among other residential developments by our client in the township; its playful semantics and defiant aesthetics can also be enjoyed literally as a caper – a prank amid the austere urban conditions of Sentul.

In all our projects, we attempt to make beautiful spaces – even with economical means. The construction is born out of a series of modest building methods, materials and structural design.

The twists and turns of the building form simply derive from the laws of physics. The floor slabs cantilever 400 millimetres (15¾ inches) at every floor, reaching the most efficient possible length before turning back to stagger in the other direction, giving the tower its zig-zag profile. The structural design is predominantly an interlocking series of reinforced-concrete vertical sheer walls and horizontal flat slabs. The rudimentary economy of the building's structure belies the challenges encountered on-site. For instance, the organic form of the towers prevented normal methods of hoisting, delivery and installation. Common construction methods were thus rethought and improvised.

The floor plate of each tower is H-shaped, with the vertical cores located along a double-loaded, naturally ventilated corridor. Special bridge units in this core that are joined to adjacent suites across the void respond to today's demands for multigenerational living. These offer prime views towards the Batu Caves – the region's tourist attraction of limestone cave temples – to the north and Kuala Lumpur's famous Petronas Twin Towers to the south.

To break the towers' monolithic surfaces and make them more porous, we weaved into the architecture a succession of fins, sky terraces and a graphical tempo of windows with the aluminium cladding of the skewed sheer walls. While the delicate details of metallic fins and edges preserve the design's proportions and geometry, the chequered aluminium panelling

Terrace units in the low-rise block of The Capers offer alternative ways of living (above). Its roof's truss system lightens the architecture (above right).

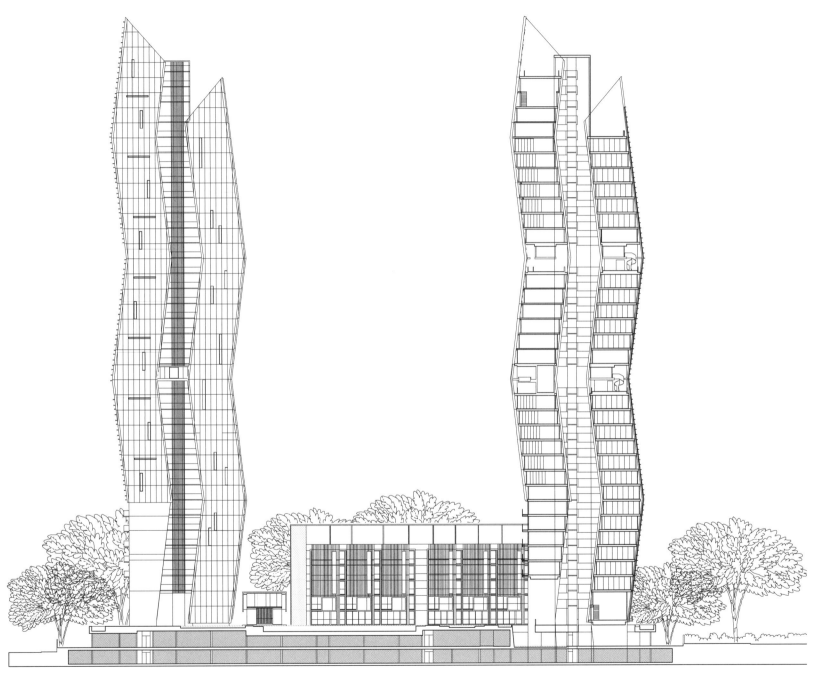

SECTION

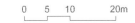

0 5 10 20m

and steel edge detailing stand out against the prevailing multicoloured and plaster-and-paint urban fabric of Sentul. The corridors, with timber-grained cement boards attenuated vertically, contrast with the sleek aluminium and steel textures. On the sky terrace floors, our penchant for surprise takes the form of vermilion spiral staircases leading to sky lounges, which inject a punch of colour into the architecture.

Lower to the ground, the architecture of the townhouses is more textural and relates to the greenery via timber-framed protrusions. In a demonstration of human-centric design, the louvred fronts of the blocks provide privacy from passers-by at the landscaped lawns, and the rooftop gardens of the upper-level duplexes present a picturesque top-down view for the units in the towers.

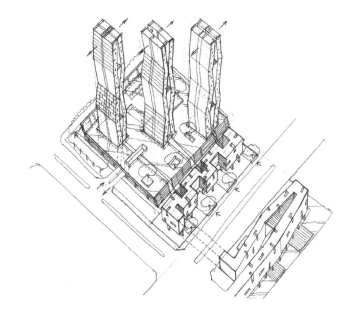

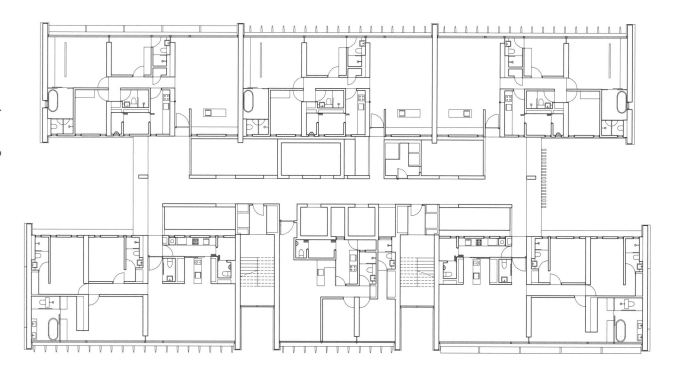

TYPICAL BLOCK PLAN

0   2   5   10m

Bridge units in the towers cater to multigenerational living and offer premium views.

The shimmering skin of d6 dematerializes the built form.

A pool at the rear offers respite (top); the mesh skins cater for vertical gardens (bottom).

The façade patterns of d7 reflect the diverse unit types.

Connecting bridges and vertical planting offer shade and relief in the courtyard of d7.

# A Practice at the Intersection

—Chan Sau Yan, Sonny

Founder and Director of CSYA, Singapore

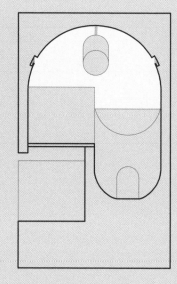

I have known TK, as he is popularly known, since he was an aspiring undergraduate of the National University of Singapore; and Rene since he came to Singapore in 1996. The founding of their eponymous RT+Q Architects brought together two individuals with a combined, complementary experience of seventy years. TK, with five decades of practice, helms the practical but necessary aspects of the business of architecture, thus enabling Rene to forge a creative studio culture environment. Both are committed and active participants in academic teaching and running intensive workshops, which include on-site visits overseas. TK has also served in various capacities in professional and government institutions. Rene has been invited to speak at forums and conferences. In 2016, he was the recipient of the prestigious President*s Design Award.

Since its inception, RT+Q has consistently produced a contemporary body of work in the modernist vein, distinguished by its vigorous architectonic design and material palette. It predominantly comprises the whole spectrum of the residential genre, ranging from the single- to the multi-family home, from low- and high-rise residences to miscellaneous commercial projects.

There is a palpable sense of adventure in the firm's diverse and innovative explorations in search of architectural identity. This can be seen in its extensive and varied repertoire of single-family residences, exemplified by the House in Three Movements (pp. 70–77), Svarga Residence (pp. 102–113) and House with a Sanctum (pp. 204–217). The contrasting styles of these three projects reflect the creative versatility and universal design sensibilities of the practice in adapting to the client's brief, the environment and the sense of place. In particular, the elegantly detailed House with a Sanctum, with its elliptical plan and armature of ancillary spaces at a tangent, is a bold and radical exposition of geometry, which fulfilled the client's brief for 'a unique residence unlike any other'.

The multi-family low-rise Shorefront (pp. 78–87) is a skilful resolution of a problem site that has a sea frontage and height constraints. These contrasting demands were ameliorated by the use of linear architectural massing and the aesthetic façade design of the blocks, which face each other across landscape terraces that lead towards the sea.

RT+Q's repertoire of high-rise residences equally reflects the confidence and creative versatility found in their single-family residential designs. The iconic imagery of The Fennel and The Capers (pp. 90–99) was achieved by the seemingly simple and deceptive design of segmentation and alternate canting of the tower and slab blocks, thereby creating a visually dynamic and robust motion compared to the static and orthodox vertical silhouette of Senopati Suites 2 and 3.

Aesthetics and materiality are defining characteristics of the practice's DNA. This can be seen in the otherwise utilitarian office blocks of d6 and d7 (pp. 90–99), which were transformed by an innovative façade fenestration and its materiality of aluminium panels and mesh screens

After twenty years of prodigious practice and multiple design awards, what will RT&Q's next phase portend?

# A Counterintuitive Partnership

—Robert Powell

Adjunct Professor, Taylor's University, Malaysia

Mindful of Rene Tan's maxim 'Think counter-intuitively,' I believe I should not simply rehearse his own, well-documented contribution to RT+Q Architects as lead designer. Instead, I will examine why his partnership with co-director Quek Tse Kwang works – and evidently works well.

TK, as he is known, is a highly respected member of the art fraternity in Singapore, and indeed Southeast Asia. Not only is he a collector of fine art but he has served as a member of the Acquisition Committee of the National Gallery Singapore as well as the Istana Art Collection Advisory Committee. He was also previously a board member of the Singapore Art Museum.

For over five decades, TK has been actively involved in the region's art scene. He has participated as an international judge for Tun Foundation Bank's annual painting competition in Myanmar. The self-confessed 'hobbyist' publisher has also produced numerous books on art in the region. These include Ahmad Zakii Anwar, *Drawings, Paintings, Prints 1991–2007* (2007) and *Min Wae Aung: Figurescape* (2011), which features the landscape works by the artist from Myanmar.

In 2010, TK published *30 Art Friends: Appreciating Southeast Asian Art*, followed up four years later with a sequel, *30 Art Friends 2: Collecting Southeast Asian Art*. The intention was to add breadth and depth to the appreciation

of art from the region in all its diversity and vitality. From well-established modern masters to young artists embarking on their careers, the two volumes showcase the calibre and appeal of artworks from Southeast Asia. We can conclude from TK's deep involvement in the arts that the architecture graduate of the University of Singapore appreciates beauty in its many forms.

TK reminds me that we met shortly after I joined the staff of the School of Architecture at the National University of Singapore. He had initiated a personal book prize for fourth-year students and I helped him to identify the recipient. That must have been around 1986.

I met Rene much later, when I published two houses designed by RT+Q in my 2009 book *Singapore Houses*. Sundridge House (House at Sundridge Park I) and Bukit Timah House (House at Dunearn) were two of Rene's earliest designs, and I learned his background in the process of interviewing him. Rene spent his childhood in Penang, and later received his BA from Yale, double-majoring in music and architecture. He was awarded his Master in Architecture from Princeton in 1990. After graduation, he worked for four years with Ralph Lerner in the USA, returning to Southeast Asia in 1996. He worked for seven years with SCDA Architects in Singapore before setting up RT+Q in 2003.

The partnership between TK and Rene was the result of a serendipitous encounter in 1994 in Syracuse, New York, and they found an easy rapport. 'Our partnership came very naturally; instinctively,' Rene recollects. 'I think we recognized each other's attributes. Architecture is such a complicated profession that one person cannot do all things – you need someone you trust.'

'It's true,' TK confirms. 'The basis of any good partnership is trust. And by relying on each other to do what's best, we found a really viable partnership.'

Like any passionate architect, Rene sees his vocation as art. 'Architecture is not just visual or verbal. It's tactile and tectonic,' he says. Yet his partner also grounds him. 'TK always reminds me, "Even the *Mona Lisa* was finished at some point, so don't overdo it". This became our mantra. Yes, make our work the best it can be, but don't get lost along the way.'

# Svarga Residence Tropicalizing the Primitive Hut

The house's tectonics abstract the roofscape of the vernacular architecture.

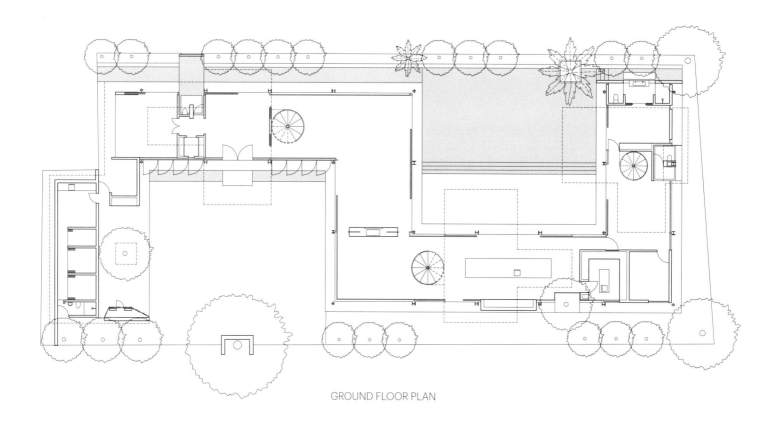

GROUND FLOOR PLAN

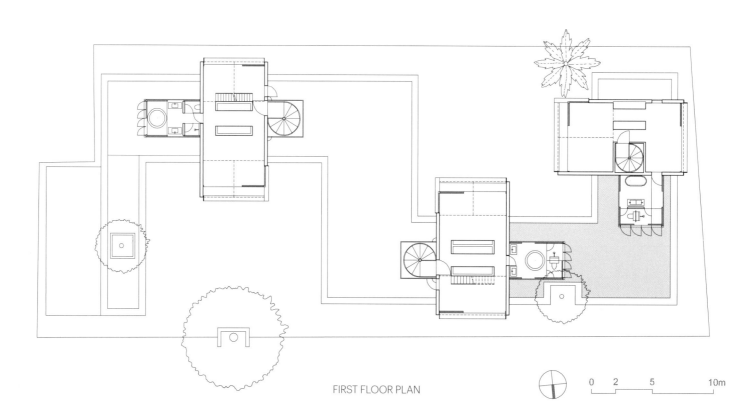

FIRST FLOOR PLAN

0    2    5    10m

Vernacular architecture comprising thatched pitched roofs is very much part of the exclusive Balinese seaside enclave of Batu Jimbar, Sanur. This holiday home for a client, for whom we had designed a house in Jakarta previously, challenged us to design a house that was attentive to the context but not subservient to it style-wise. It led to a search for a new domestic idiom. The conventional notions of the home, the house and dwelling were rethought (the typical courtyard house dismantled), re-examined (the vernacular thatched roof element substituted), and reconstructed (steel was used extensively in place of conventional structural material) into a new image and living environment.

The client requested a beach house with Balinese elements on this plot without actual views of the sea. The brief was also packed with other requests: one daughter wanted her own villa while another desired to camp outdoors, and the wife wished for every aspect of the home to be superlative in size and experience. Out of these, we aimed to create Balinese spaces, rather than Balinese buildings, to avoid pastiche. This translated namely to pavilion-like rooms fused with their surroundings, the use of natural materials and a strong sense of craftsmanship.

Formally, the house reads as a trio of barn-like structures. Each has a projecting bathroom unit and they are perched atop an S-shaped base – an arrangement that combines three 'Primitive Huts' (see below) with a Barcelona Pavilion (referencing Mies van der Rohe's iconic project for expressing simplicity and clarity). On the ground floor, the meandering plan loops spaces into a seamless trajectory in order to foster communal living. The winding gesture birthed two courtyards. The first is public-facing, housing a driveway at the entrance. The second, more private courtyard contains the swimming pool, surrounded by the living, dining and guestrooms.

Three spiral staircases lead to the three bedrooms on the first floor, which are self-sufficient units with a loft. They sit among grass and water bodies that give the illusion of the piano nobile as a reconstituted ground plane. It was important that the feeling of water permeate the house as the plot does not face the coast. Each 'barn' is identified with different cladding too. While the parents' block stands out with aluminium sheets, the other two blend into the bucolic backdrop of nature and traditional architecture. One is wrapped with timber shingles and the other is clad with recycled marine timber planks from boats that bear the stains of their aquatic past. The abstraction of pitched-roof elements engages with the context yet also singles them out.

The narrow road leading to the site meant that large elements such as the main staircase and steel structure were constructed off-site, and then shipped and assembled on-site. The different building practices in Bali compared to Singapore also forced more intuitive construction methods. Construction drawings were redrawn according to site conditions, details rethought with local expertise, and materials substituted owing to site limitations. This process of designing – or rather, redesigning – on the ground enhanced rather than derailed both process and products. For instance, timber scaffolding that was to be discarded was upcycled into trellised screens for the first-floor bathrooms. Trees that stood in the way of the original plan were accommodated as part of the building, bridging dwelling and land. These measures aligned with sustainable architecture too. The house is designed to harness natural light and ventilation, while the garden and pool on the roof lower ambient temperatures.

The reinterpretation of the traditional Balinese villa stimulated a new tributary in our exploration of form, grounded in the ideology of the Primitive Hut, conceptualized by 18th-century French architecture theorist Marc-Antoine Laugier, and encapsulated in the simple form of a pitched roof, beams and supports. The archetype led to further adaptation in later projects, such as House with Bridges and House with Shadows (see pp. 144 and 174), giving birth to a new language for our works that is at once traditional and modern.

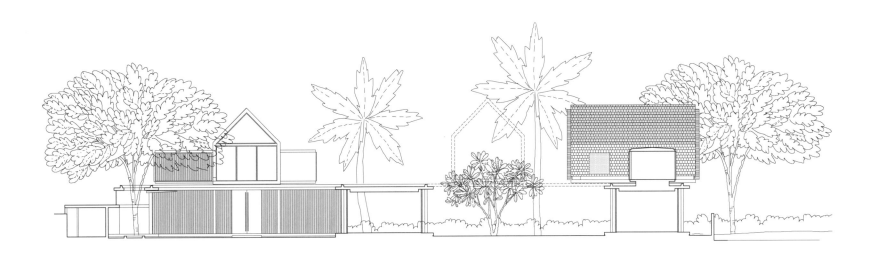

SECTION

0   2   5   10m

The edge profiles of the 'barns' explore various detailing expressions, and timber parts soften the character of the steel columns (above left and middle).

The separate entities of the 'barns' allow for pure material expression.

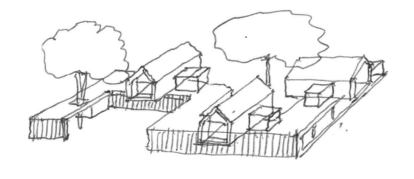

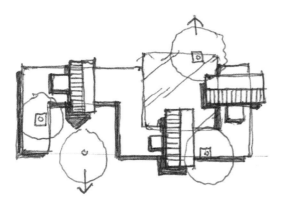

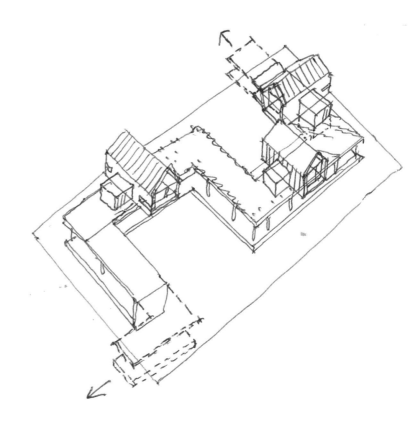

The cantilevered profiles of the upper blocks give the architecture a sense of lightness.

Extending the bathrooms out of the sleeping areas maintains the intimate scale of the 'barn' units.

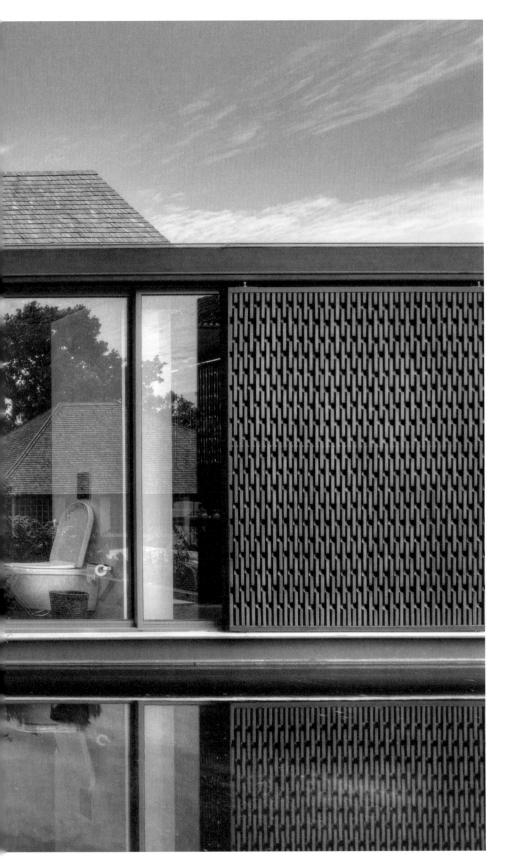

An inclined steel plate functions as a water spout in the guest bathroom (top); the master bathroom (bottom).

An internal courtyard is formed from the ground floor's S-shaped form.

# House on a Prairie
A modern vernacular house

The main house is raised 4 metres (13 feet) above the entry level, following the natural terrain.

A house owner's brief is typically what gives a property its distinctive qualities. Hence, how should one approach a project where there is no owner? This was the challenge we faced in designing this project for a local developer. Our strategy for such developments that need to appeal to a wide range of potential buyers is to reduce architecture to its bare minimum considerations of proportions, skin and bones. The underlying aim of the tectonic experiment for this house was to create a 'modern Primitive Hut', inspired by Marc-Antoine Laugier's concept of basic shelter. Our name for the project, which conjures imagery of a simple dwelling on a vast, flat, treeless grassland, also reflects how its design optimizes the land rather than maximizes it – a rarity in the dense residential urbanscape of Singapore, and the result of an enlightened client.

The massing of the two-storey house is kept low-key, and appears to rise to only a single storey thanks to the hilly site that is about 4 metres (13 feet) above street level. The driveway is placed on the lower part of the land, leading into a grand basement entrance. This preserves as much land as possible for the elevated ground floor – the piano nobile – where the communal spaces and bedrooms are placed along the sprawling garden, whose vistas beyond comprise spectacular, uninterrupted views of the hills and greenery. Despite being tucked underground, the basement too has abundant light as we opened it up to the equally long driveway.

On the ground floor, the spaces are organized into a clear L-shaped form. Common areas line up on the arm parallel to the driveway, while the other arm comprises the master bedroom suite, looking over the swimming pool and large garden, and three bedrooms housed in concrete cubes that extend towards the rear. The latter offers intimate views of a line of bamboo plants that serve as a privacy screen. A sliver of landscaping is also created in the voids between each of the blocks, with narrow windows looking out to small bamboo gardens, reflecting our belief in integrating pleasant elements into daily living regardless of scale and hierarchy of space. The form of the boxes extends beyond the glass doors to form a portal, which both frames the landscaping and becomes a buffer from climatic elements.

The 'modern Primitive Hut' idea formulates architecturally into a minimal physical structure that is essentially a rudimentary post-and-beam

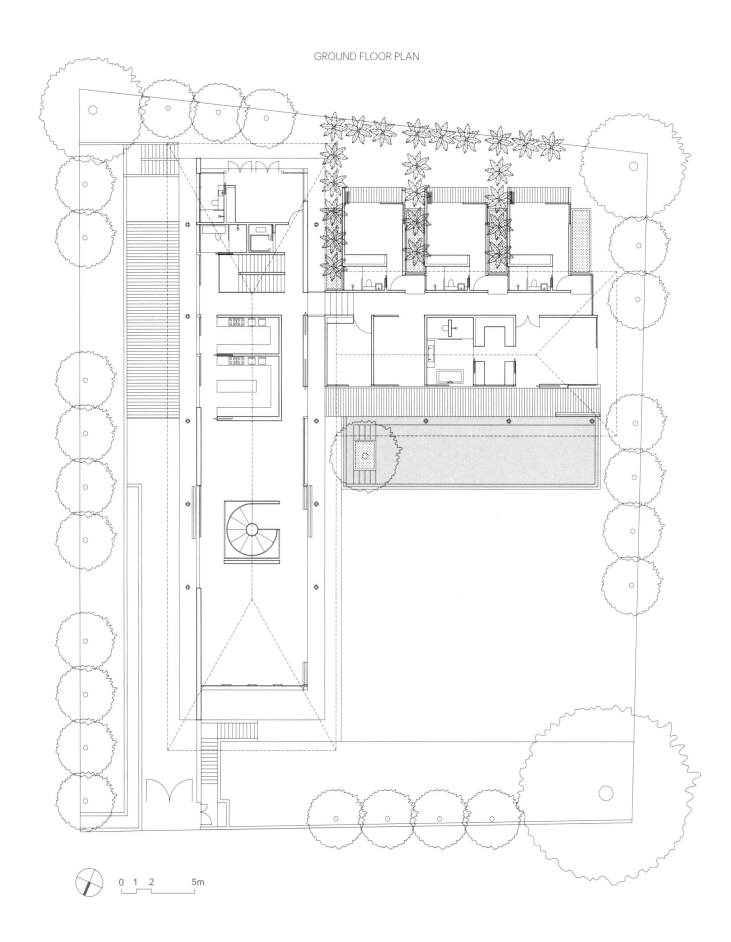

0  1  2        5m

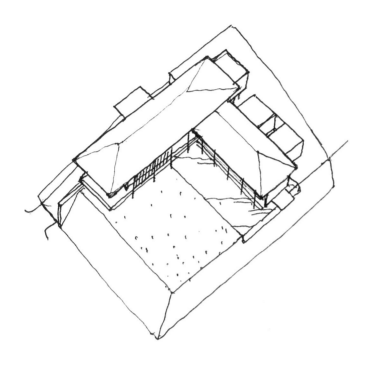

method of lightweight elements, such as steel, aluminium and glass. These materials render the building transparent and airy, allowing it to touch the land delicately. While it is simple, much thought is given to detailing. For example, the slender and elegant columns are made of four L-shaped steel brackets, into which we designed lighting that subtly illuminates the corridors. In another example, the block with the common spaces is elevated slightly to read as a floating volume on a bed of crushed gravel. Both blocks are capped by low hip roofs. These literal symbols of shelter extend far out as pragmatic solutions to the tropical heat, glare and rain. Another device for privacy and climatic mitigation is the sliding timber screens that are employed generously as part of the building's skin. The density and intimate scale of timber parts create a texture like knitted fabric. It is a tribute to German architect Gottfried Semper's thesis in *The Four Elements of Architecture* (1851) that attributes weaving as the origin of enclosures.

Besides Western influences, the house embraces in all its parts a contemporary interpretation of the tropical vernacular, such as the Malay kampong house (a timber home on stilts with a post-and-lintel structure, louvred timber windows and wooden walls) and our Black and White House, a later iteration of the former, which is a concrete construction with louvred windows raised on concrete plinths. Through a process of abstraction, we continually seek to bridge tradition with modernity in the belief that they have a symbiotic responsibility in the conception of new and relevant forms.

House on a Prairie

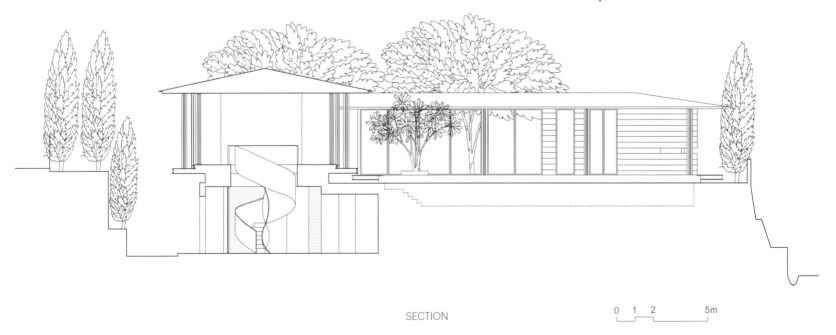

SECTION

0   1   2        5m

Private and public spaces are distinguished by the two arms of the L-shaped house.

120     A sculptural spiral staircase dramatically marks the entry to the sprawling house above.

The bedrooms are designed as private sanctuaries facing a rear garden. 121

122    The sleek edges of the roof and floor emphasize the horizontal lines of the architecture.

The master bathroom (top); and the raised living-room block (bottom). 123

# House of the Connoisseur

Reinventing a shophouse structure and skin

An open-air courtyard forms the threshold between the original conserved block and the new rear extension.

Shophouses were once abundant in early Singapore. These terraced houses are a local appropriation of similar typologies brought over by Chinese immigrants, and typically feature terracotta roof tiles and shuttered French windows, fronted by so-called 'five-foot ways' – covered corridors that thread houses into a row while sheltering pedestrians from rain and sun. Many have been demolished because of Singapore's post-independence *tabula rasa* strategies, but about 6,500 of them have been conserved and are now coveted for their heritage and their unique spatial qualities. One example is a 1920s shophouse that we worked on that used to belong to the late Ng Eng Teng, a local sculptor known for his figurative public sculptures. Its ornate façade articulations reflect the neighbourhood of Joo Chiat, an eastern enclave in Singapore that was once home to a vibrant Eurasian and Peranakan (Straits Chinese) community.

While in decent condition, the interiors of the shophouse – a warren of small rooms – were unsuitable for its new owners. They wanted a more open dwelling in which to bring up their young family and host large gatherings. The brief was for the design to integrate with the cultural context and to explore the sustainable approach of infusing new life into an old building of historical value.

We dutifully conserved the front façade as mandated by the local authorities, retaining and restoring architraves, relief mouldings and panelled brickwork columns. New timber doors and windows were also installed based on original designs. The delicate exterior belies our transmutation of the interior into an open, fluid space that overcomes the limited exposure to light, ventilation and views within the 23.5-metre-deep (77-foot) space flanked on both sides by party walls. Our design intervenes with this space in between the walls to expand it and afford it an engagement with the outdoors, while carefully ensuring a harmonious dialogue of old and new, in both the design and the construction processes.

Tectonically, this 'in-between' theme translates into an assortment of 'infill' components, each with specific roles of bridging, screening, erasure and addition. Together, they break the monotony of traversing the long plan. The most major infill

The owners requested that the courtyard remain exposed to the elements.

GROUND FLOOR PLAN

FIRST FLOOR PLAN

ATTIC PLAN

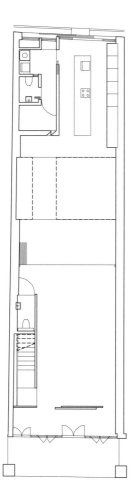

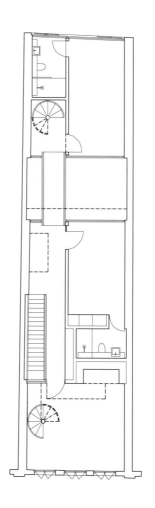

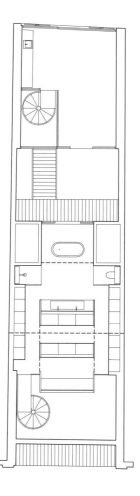

0  1  2        5m

is paradoxically an extraction – a central void that alters the house's linear trajectory into an assemblage of parts. Natural light washes down the off-form concrete walls of this courtyard, bringing awareness of nature's shifting dispositions. It is enclosed at the rear with a new block – itself another infill – that expands the size of the house from 309 to 343 square metres (3,326 to 3,692 square feet). Although height controls permit a maximum of five storeys for the additional block, we opted for a proportionately friendlier massing of three storeys distributed among a variety of ceiling heights, including a vertiginous entertainment room in the attic. Here is where the client – a connoisseur of whiskies and other fine interests – can showcase his collections.

Other infills comprise interior architectural elements, designed as either secondary spaces (wardrobes, glass boxes and guest bathroom) or circulation spines (a bridge connecting the old and new volumes, as well as vertical access). These parts exist as fixed elements within larger zones that have been spatially or visually amplified with transparent or porous skins. For example, 3-metre-wide (10-foot) pivoting glass doors fuse the courtyard with the living room and kitchen on each side. The rear façade is also wrapped with an expanded metal mesh screen that channels breezes through the building while weaving a connection between the house and its neighbourhood.

The mesh screen is unapologetically modern in outlook and gives the house the aspect of a lantern after dusk. Its sliding mechanism means that the visage is ever-mutating, playing out like an urban theatre to reflect the domestic situations at different times of day. The screen's design takes its cue from the Peranakan culture's love of detail and adornment. The diagrid (diagonal grid) pattern, pleated and oriented to stiffen the material for strength, also filters light and vistas without compromising airflow. From an urban planning viewpoint, we wanted the house to look good not just from the front but also from the back because of this typology's rare street presence. Within the house, timber screens with an equally textured pattern demarcate the thresholds between the foyer and living room. It continues inwards as a tactile, shadowed casing, giving beauty to utilitarian needs such as a staircase, storage space and guest bathroom.

By harnessing the unique traits of history and modernity, the house accords the occupants new, layered encounters in their daily lives.

House of the Connoisseur

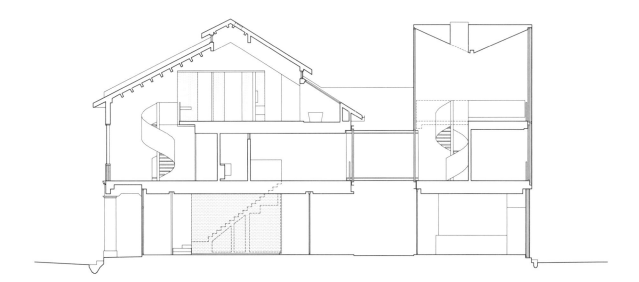

SECTION

0  1  2        5m

Sliding mesh screens open the house to the back lane, which functions as an informal play space for the children (above left, middle and opposite).

'Infill' study above master bedroom (above); the kitchen (middle) is visually linked to the central courtyard and private back lane, making it feel larger.

The decorative streetscape at the front.

# Art Collector's House
House for art, house as art

A formal entry both connects and distinguishes the blocks for two different generations.

A two-storey art wall in the living room offers a changing backdrop.

Another variation of a multigenerational house but brought closer to home is this dwelling belonging to our co-founder TK Quek. He had brought up his children in the original building, which was of a Balinese design popular in the 1980s and had a large front lawn. The redesign was to accommodate the expanded family. This comprises his younger son and director at the firm, Jonathan Quek, who is now married with a family, together with his older son when he visits from abroad. Like 'friendly neighbours', the layout gives the individual families autonomy as well as shared experiences through the use of common facilities such as the swimming pool.

The clear demarcation of wings and provision of separate living and dining rooms respect the boundaries of the two households by reducing pressure for constant interaction. The house also had to integrate TK's extensive art collection, which reveals itself to the residents as they move through the property, the artworks functioning as markers of place, time and memory.

The atmosphere of the house is defined by the relationship between solid and void, mass and ground. The spaces are distributed into three volumes organized around a large void in the form of the swimming pool, like a pinwheel. Two of the volumes are longitudinal and positioned along the site's length – one parallel to the driveway for TK and his wife and the other stretching towards the rear for Jonathan's family. Both are hinged at their opposite ends by the formal entrance, thus maintaining unblocked views, cross-ventilation and a level of privacy from each other. Their longer elevations oriented north–south reduce solar heat gain. We counterintuitively placed TK's block right next to a high-rise condominium development at the site's northern boundary and found this to be advantageous as the swimming pool and the development's landscaping buffer his block from it.

The entrance portal, fronted with two black pools and timber screens, presents a formal prelude. Behind it is a veranda, where a bronze sculpture of a winged man by Spanish artist Jesús Curiá gives dramatic pause. As one turns right, a double-storey living room is a grand introduction to TK's portion of the property. A family room on the first floor overlooks this expanse. On it, a rotund fellow perched precariously on a ladder – a playful work by Chinese sculptor Mu Boyan – reflects TK's penchant for the whimsical in his art collecting.

In this living room, a 7-metre-high (23-foot) wall is fronted with overlapping gridded metal panels that can be mechanically raised or lowered to display different artworks. This is a highlight of the space, and lets TK enjoy and showcase his art collection without being limited by the number of walls in the house.

While TK's wing possesses a certain grandeur, Jonathan's is more intimate and tailored to a young family. The ground floor has an open plan for living and dining, and the kitchen with a bar counter facing the swimming pool facilitates casual gatherings around food and outdoor play.

The guest wing at the rear is characterized by a cloak of green foliage that compensates for the reduction of the lawn after the redevelopment. Architecture and landscape synthesize to create a sculptural element in line with the house's art focus. Strategically placed apertures in the other two wings afford the residents picturesque vistas of this art of nature. Materials such as glass, timber, travertine and lava stone are composed on the elevations like pieces of an abstract canvas. All this is capped with a generous aluminium roof overhang that completes the house's lucid tectonic quality.

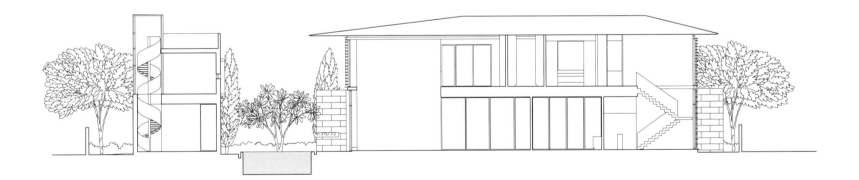

SECTION

0  1  2      5m

An alternative entrance at the right fronts the driveway to provide an artful welcome.

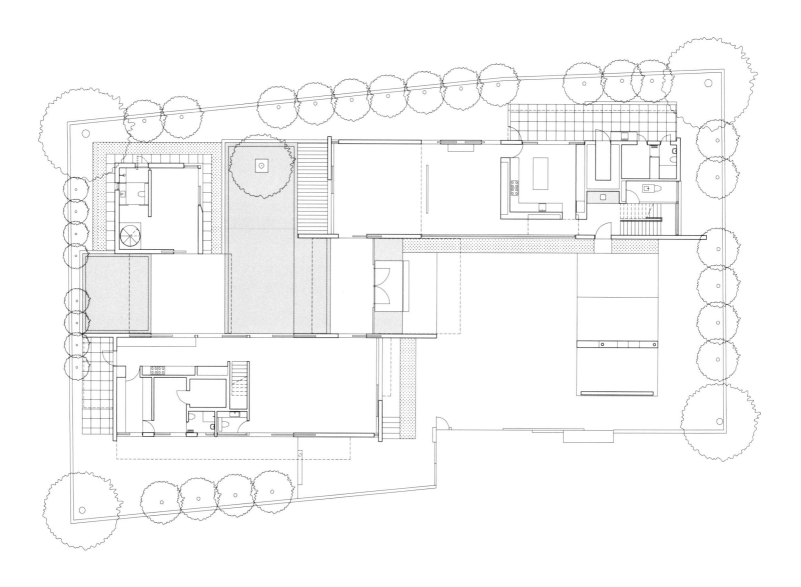

GROUND FLOOR PLAN

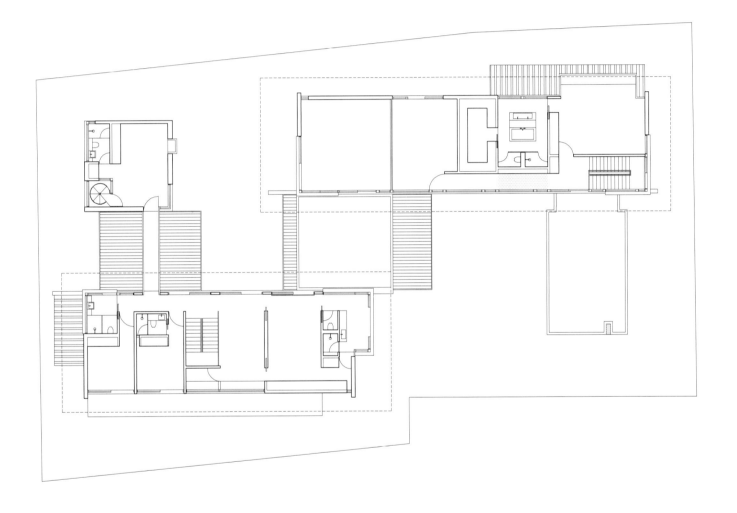

FIRST FLOOR PLAN

0  1  2          5m

The use of lava stone gives a sense of gravitas to the ground floor.

The swimming pool at the entrance offers a tranquil introduction to the house.

Aluminium louvres temper the heat and glare entering the double-height living room.

A green wall offers the other blocks an aesthetically appealing view.

# House with Bridges

Bridges as a topographical response

The client's preference for a dark palette creates a subdued foil to the greenery.

The concept of bridges takes on multiple interpretations in this house, linking internal spaces as well as habitat and landscape. It was born of a complicated site with a 14-metre-high (46-foot) reinforced-concrete retaining wall. The client saw potential in the escarpment as a vertical garden to indulge her love of greenery, but the site conditions rendered it dangerous and unbuildable for the most part. To add to the challenges, she required the already tight site to house three generations, each with substantial private living requirements.

We responded with a design that is encountered vertically over four storeys, rising in tandem with the stepped slope that backs the house. This allowed us to explore and exploit the potential of the architectural section. In plan, a simple L-shaped volume forms a central void with the retaining wall. The front portion contains the common spaces and loft bedrooms for the two sons, while the grandfather's room, the master bedroom and the study are stacked in the rear barn. The basement merges with the road level to house a sheltered car park and a guest bathroom.

Domestic events unfold throughout the house via a series of contrasting encounters – double-height spaces, mezzanines, light-filled corners, bridges, decks, and open and contained realms. Another important element is the staircases, which help in navigating the spatial strata.

Excluding an outdoor staircase, there are four indoors, each with a unique design. A compact spiral staircase in each of the sons' bedrooms links entertaining and sleeping zones. In the rear block, a large spiral staircase tunnels up from the ground floor to the attic. A final staircase – a crisp Corten steel construct – at the front of the house leading from the basement to the first floor is encased in glass like an exhibit.

In this house, we designed three bridges that cantilever playfully towards the vertical garden. They reach close to but never touch the rock escarpments for fear of instability and damage to the capricious wall. More balconies than bridges, they enable the occupants to probe the

Portals and fenestrations become avenues for tectonic expression.

The pitched roofs uplift the interiors of the attic spaces to counterbalance the dark palette.

ambiguous realms of architecture and landscape in a dramatic process that excites the senses. The first bridge extends from the bedroom of one of the sons as a Corten steel volume whose lightweight metal mesh floor offers a precarious experience. The second bridge, hovering above the attic study, has walls of expanded metal mesh and a glass ceiling that dematerializes the edge between shelter and tree foliage.

The third bridge is an extension of the attic study and serves as the client's personal retreat for creative pursuits. Designed like a glasshouse with a transparent pitched roof, it pays homage to a similar space in the client's childhood home. The original rustic timber floorboards were even transported into this space as a piece of memory. It is a miniature version of the house's overall form, defined as two distinct 'barns' crowned by aluminium pitched roofs and walled with timber.

The cantilevering of spaces and close connection between nature and architecture carry through to the interiors. The counter of the dry kitchen is designed to reach out of the window to become a floating planter box. Likewise, the guest bathroom's washbasin extends out to the courtyard as a visual anchor to be admired from the upper levels. At the front of the house, the swimming pool is also articulated as a raised object, with a presence on both the basement and the ground floor.

The cohesive architecture of the house belies the many challenges that had to be overcome in design, land use, spatial organization and construction. A light construction approach was taken to the structural design for safety. Above ground, steel was primarily employed for its lightness and speed of construction. Heavy equipment was not allowed on-site so as to maintain the stability of the existing slopes; and at times the compact land size, odd shape and difficult access prevented multiple trades from being carried out concurrently. During construction, the discovery of topographical discrepancies even threatened to reduce the ground-floor space. However, we turned it into a design opportunity by integrating the slope into the living room as an organic feature wall.

In sum, the house represents our continual search for novel ways of circumventing the constraints of density and intensification that are common in land-scarce Singapore. The nooks and crannies formed in the planning and design offer the family places to perch, shelter, ponder and experience myriad ways of occupation at human scale.

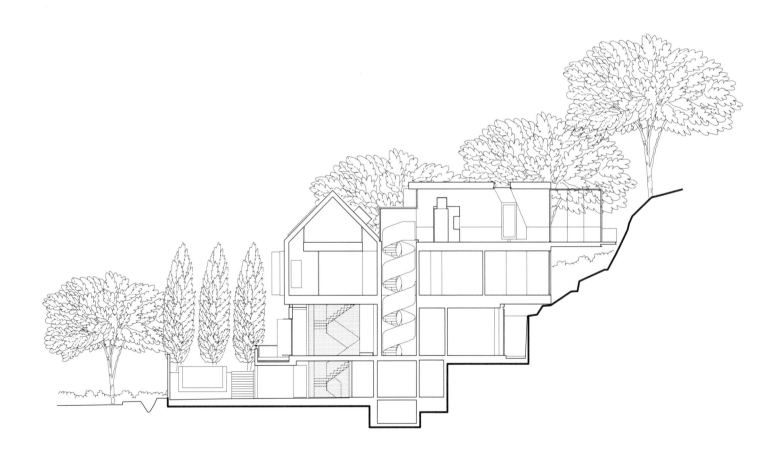

SECTION

0 1 2 5m

Screens, bridges, skylights and courtyards invite the landscape to participate in the architecture (this page).

Raising the swimming pool lightens the off-form concrete structure's mass.

Rethinking the Tropical House    20 Years of RT+Q Architects

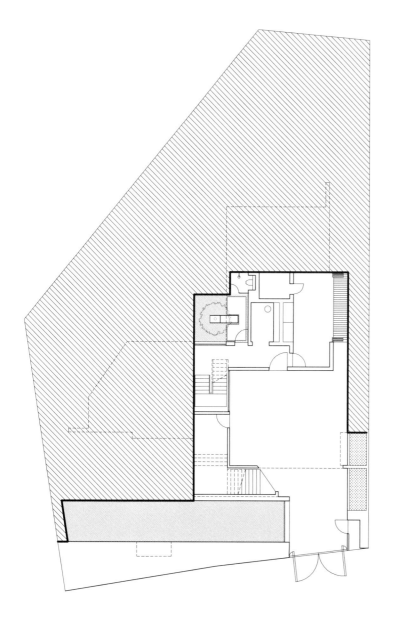

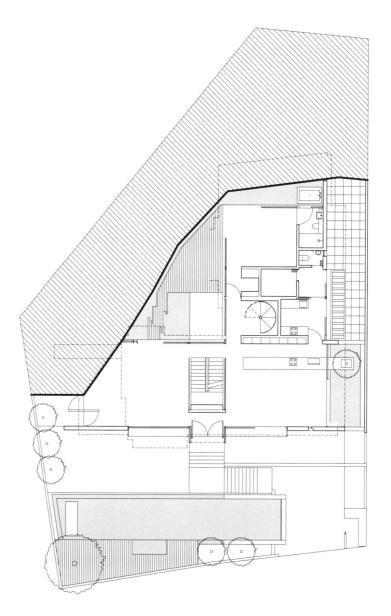

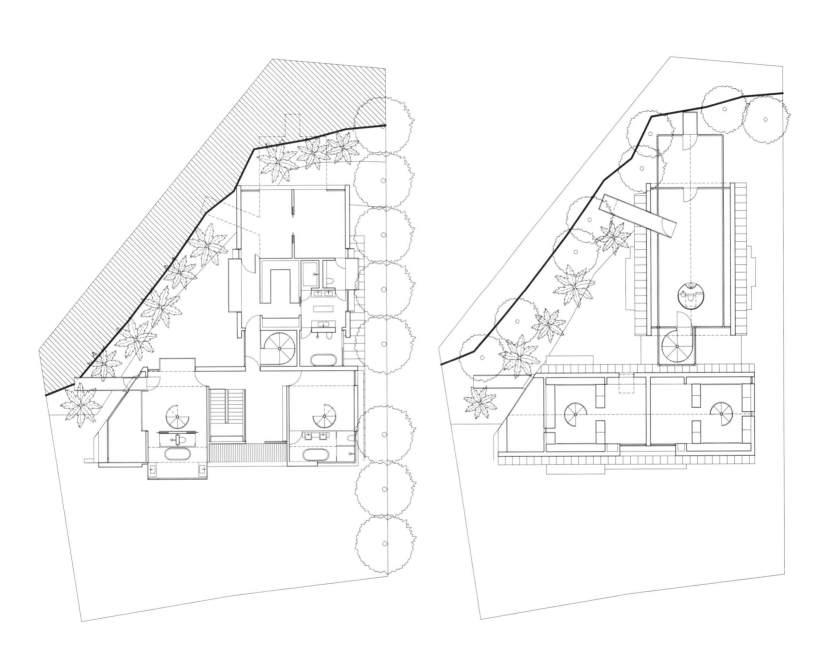

**House with Bridges**

0 1 2      5m

152    The guest bathroom's washbasin is designed as a monolithic, cantilevering volume (above).

A spiral staircase in the bedroom of one of the sons (middle); and the main staircase at the front of the house (above).  153

# House off Cluny

The many ways to frame a view

Delicate timber fins soften the forms of the living room and first floor.

The experience in this house plays out in slow reveal. The first main encounter is a grand tectonic expression composed of tall portals. The second comes after the main door as a panoramic impression of water and nature in the form of the swimming pool and a sprawling garden. This sequencing was motivated by the site's pentagon shape, which is narrower at the entrance and fans out towards the rear. We also wished to address the client's request for a large garden, which we achieved with the sizable lawn tucked away from the street view, as suited for children to play in as for garden parties. The lawn is aligned with the neighbour's garden to optimize the sense of open space, while the ample greenery references the lushness of the nearby Singapore Botanic Gardens, a UNESCO World Heritage Site.

Inspired by Prussian architect Karl Friedrich Schinkel's country houses in 19th-century Berlin, which propagated the neoclassical courtyard house, we pursued an architectural strategy of framing views. The plan is a simple C shape, which results in a central courtyard containing the swimming pool. Its open side faces the lawn, offering expansive views across the land. The private quarters are contained in two long blocks – a one-storey and a two-storey volume – that overlap perpendicularly in section. Glass doors on the long elevations facing the pool and deck invite easy access to the outdoors.

In contrast to the horizontality of this massing is the double-height living room, contained in an inverted U-shaped shell that emphasizes its verticality and distinguishes it as a public entertainment zone. Entering the house from the road requires a descent into the entrance foyer under a glass bridge that joins this block with the other two – a gesture that clearly distinguishes private and public areas. The compression of space expands exuberantly into the living room, with the change in atmosphere accentuated by the shift in materials from grey stone and timber to pure white Statuario marble cladding the floor and walls. A spiral staircase cascading from the glass bridge allows secondary access into the living room from the private quarters, its curves interrupting the streamlined architecture.

An assortment of devices is used to lighten the monumentality of the massing. Steel was used for exposed structural members such as free-standing columns to perpetuate a sense

The elevated bedrooms have direct views to the garden.

of lightness and clarity of structure. The living-room block is visually 'freed' from the ground with panels of glass at the base, while an array of slot windows punctures the walls and ceiling, mitigating the scale of the large expanse of walls. Timber 'eyelash' fins soften the edges of the block's shorter ends.

On the first floor, the glass bridge extrudes out of the end wall insouciantly, terminating in a Juliet balcony overlooking the landscaping. The bold gesture is echoed across the pool with a grey box containing the pool shower, which cantilevers over the lawn. The relationship between architecture and the land is intricately intertwined, and is directly translated to the user experience in many instances. One such example is an intimate stepped garden capping one side of the living room, which gently negotiates the terrain that

dips 2 metres (6½ feet) from the site's entrance. The steps in the garden double as seating for quiet conversation or for observing other people during a party. Here, the framing of activities occurs both ways.

Another important aspect of the project is the deference to sustainable living. We oriented the main wing east–west, with the longer glazed elevations facing north–south. All the rooms in the house are designed with the option of natural ventilation. On the façade, protruding steel tips protect window openings from rain, heat and glare, and a serried band of timber brise-soleil functions as privacy and sun shields for the west-facing master bedroom on the first floor. The porosity and other attributes, such as deep overhangs, make tropical living easy in this house.

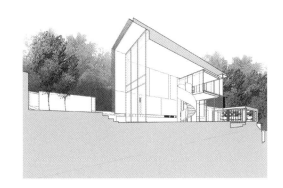

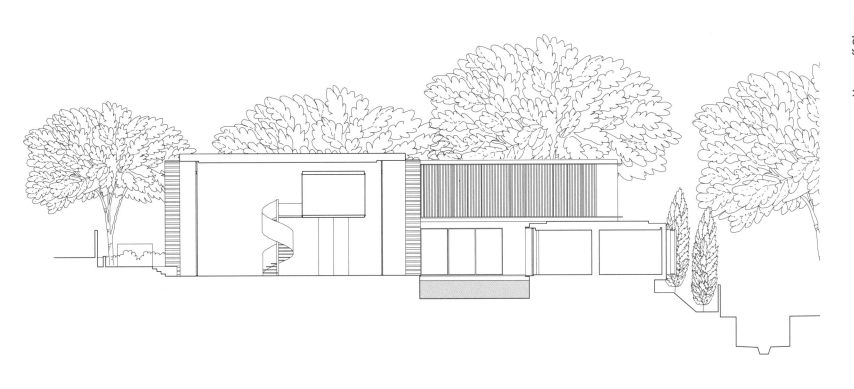

SECTION

0 1 2 5m

The architectural components define the pool and frame the garden.

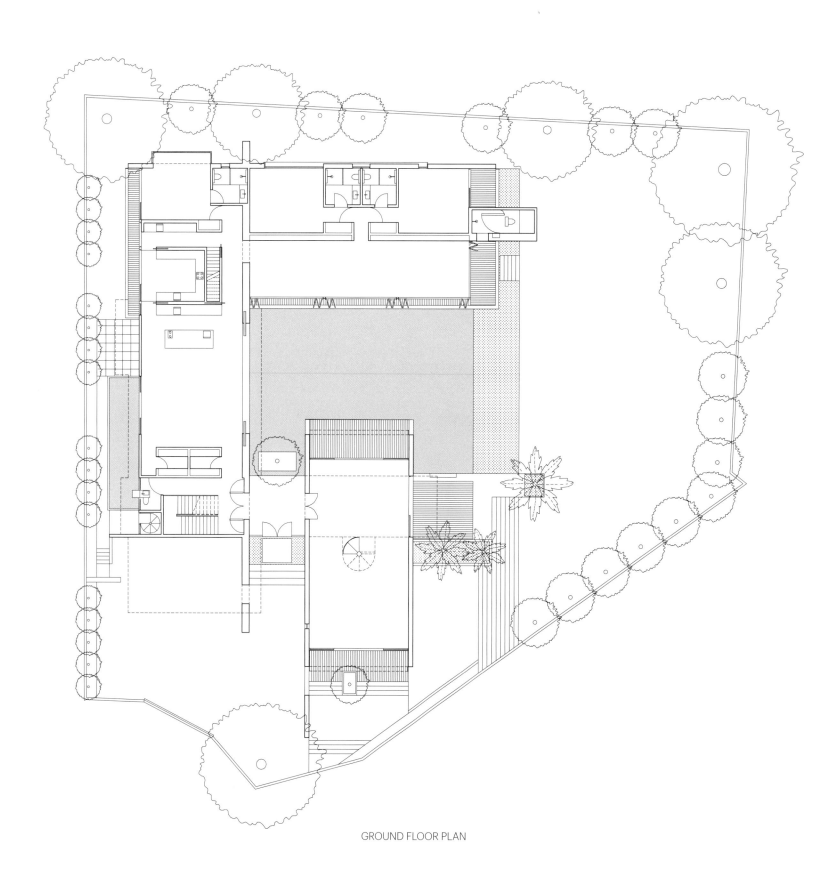

GROUND FLOOR PLAN

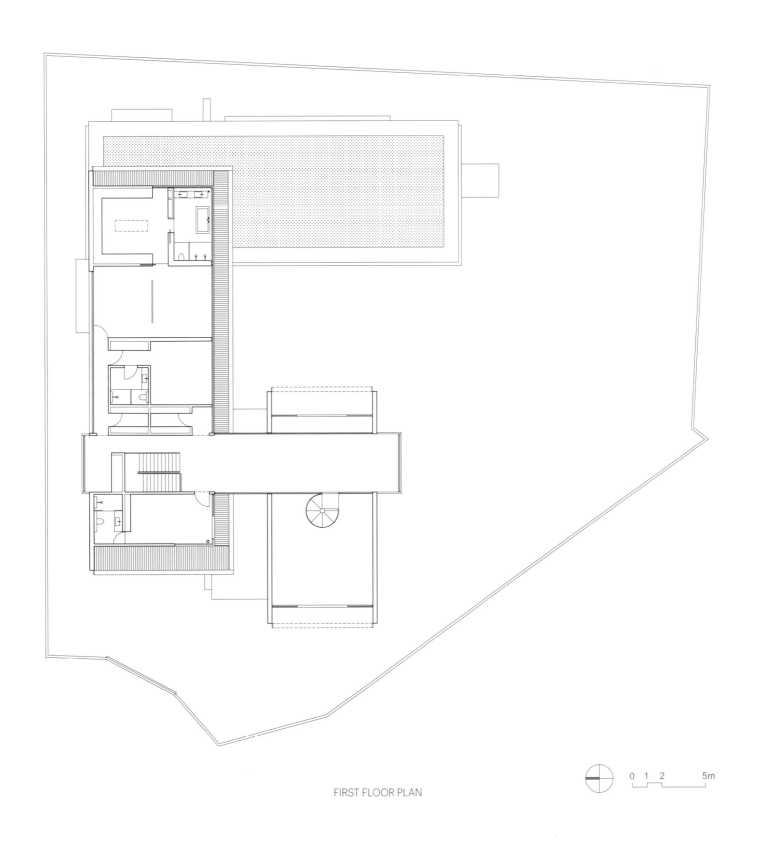

FIRST FLOOR PLAN

0  1  2        5m

162    A glass bridge threads through and connects the living-room block to the private zone.

A spiral staircase leads from the living room to the study area.

# House of the Twins

An old and new block shape an 'impluvium'

The new additions are designed to quietly integrate with the existing house.

Addition and alteration works are always complex to manoeuvre. Depending on the direction, the fate of a building's established narrative lies in the hands of the architect. House of the Twins is a pivotal project where we gleaned the rewards of a concise and simple approach.

The original one-storey house is set in the middle of a large garden on a 1,858-square-metre (20,000-square-foot) plot of land. Its design was sensitive to the environment but had been altered by previous owners, who conjoined parts in an arbitrary manner. The rustic palette was also tired. After some deliberation with the new owners, we decided to retain the existing structure rather than build anew, and to expand it for the family of four with twin daughters. The new functions include a guestroom, family library, music room, master bedroom, service wing, kitchen, daughters' bedrooms and four-car garage. Our manoeuvres keep in mind the original building's charming scale and one-storey level that is essential in giving every room a sense of closeness to the earth.

The process was akin to a surgical procedure – systematic and purposeful. We cut away the house's deformed parts, such as the timber pavilions that were comfortable but dated. We also restored defining features, including the exposed timber rafters and window frames. The terracotta roof tiles were replaced with more tempered grey clay versions, while the exterior patterned walls and columns were levelled off and painted white to articulate their essential structural role.

What remained was a neat L-shaped block, with which we mirrored a new L-shaped spine in a manner that complemented rather than overwhelmed the original spaces. This 'twinning' scheme is reflected in the house's name (coincidentally, the couple also has twin daughters). The negative space in between old and new parts becomes a water courtyard, like the impluvium (rainwater capture pool) of an ancient Roman house. It serves as the new centre of the house, distributing light, ventilation and a sense of tranquillity to surrounding spaces. In terms of the spatial distribution, the old block contains more formal functions such as the living room, dining room and study-cum-music-room, linked through the original arched portals. The other spaces are distributed through the new block.

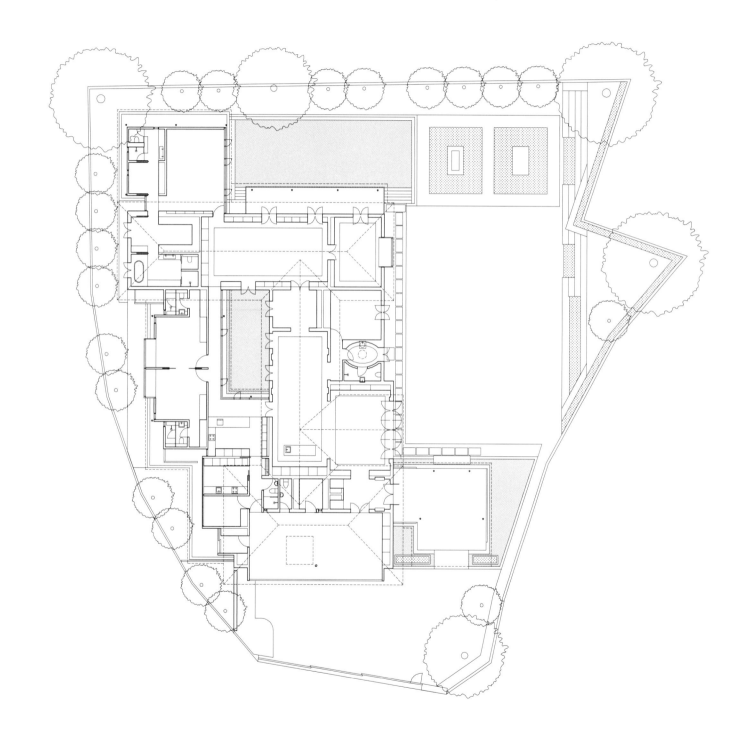

GROUND FLOOR PLAN

The original house.

We replaced the two existing timber pavilions with an enclosed master bedroom overlooking the pool and an open-walled pavilion at the main entrance that serves as a semi-formal lounge area. For a more effective spatial relationship servicing the routines of leaving or arriving home, we carved a garage from some rooms at the front of the house that now links seamlessly to the back-of-house spaces and kitchen.

While we respected the character of the original house, we disrupted it with an element of surprise. An ovoid guest bathroom between the guestroom and living room breaks the predictable, orthogonal momentum of the plan. The shape is emphasized by walls panelled fully in timber veneer, except at four vertices: the guest bathroom's curved door into the dining room on one side; double French doors with views and access to the garden on the other;

the doors to the toilet and shower area tucked into residual space between curved and straight walls; and the washbasin atop a marble plinth. An oculus inspired by Baroque chapels brings directional light into the bathroom and tells the time of day like a sundial.

To differentiate between old and new parts, a minimal tectonic language was deployed for the latter. It is manifested in low profiles, flat roofs, slim columns and light steel structures, in contrast to the old block's brick-and-plaster shell and pitched roofs. These elements are harmonized with an all-white aesthetic. Around the house, we kept the landscaping equally simple, as the owner wanted an uncluttered green lawn good to kick a ball in. It reflects the House of the Twins' embodiment of an elementary way of living – one that the owners were enlightened enough to seek.

SECTION

0  1  2      5m

The entrance pavilion is designed as an intimate space to enjoy the garden and receive guests.

The high ceilings of the original house were retained. 169

A water court was inserted between the old and new wings.

The existing swimming pool was deepened and enlarged.

172    The ovoid-shaped guest bathroom has two entrances, so guests can directly access the garden during gatherings.

Additions are subtly knitted into the original fabric to preserve the existing house's elegance.

174    A shadowed box encases the dining room in the daughter's wing, while the main block's entry is a theatre of light and shadow.

# House with Shadows

A theatre of light, shade and shadow

An intimate garden at the front is a prelude to the house's union with the landscaping.

In the design of this house, the spaces came before the forms. Whereas landscaping is often an afterthought in the conventional design process, we worked with the client's son-in-law, a landscape architect, from the initial planning of the project to create distinctive outdoor spaces that play a big part in shaping the internal experiences.

The over 4,800-square-metre (51,670-square-foot) site is combined from two plots, each housing a bungalow. The client purchased both plots, and subdivided the overall plot into three parcels. In the middle parcel, he built a home for his wife and himself, as well as their daughter and her family. On the flanking plots, he developed houses for rent – both variations of the home in the centre.

The multigenerational needs of his house required the calibration of communal and personal spaces. This is reflected in the massing, with the shared spaces arranged along a central spine. Two wings extend from it. On one side is a self-sufficient block for the daughter's family, its long elevation parallel to the street. The other is a modestly sized block housing the humbler needs of the client and his wife.

The resulting parti diagram embodying the key concept reads as an asymmetrical T shape in the plan, with the negative spaces between and around these three volumes filled with courtyards, pools or gardens to bring visual and thermal relief to the interiors. As the plot is on a slope, we raised the more important spaces above street level to give them a better vantage point and privacy. We tucked the garage into the basement at street level, which released more space for landscaping above.

A flight of outdoor steps that threads up from the roadside entrance to the ground-floor entrance positions the garden experience as a pivotal part of the arrival sequence. Three outdoor landscape concepts generate meaningful spaces between the buildings. The first is an intimate 'secret garden' fronting the street, curtained with the foliage of two mature trees transplanted from the roadside. The second is a water garden in the form of a swimming pool edged by plants, poised in the centre of the site. The third embodies the stillness and tranquillity of a Japanese Zen garden with a pond, which the client can enjoy from the sheltered patio outside his bedroom.

The double-pitched profiles of the common block and the daughter's block abstract the Primitive Hut analogy with a profile that relates more closely to the classic barn form than the regional vernacular type. Instead of an overhang, the roofline turns sharply to merge with the walls but stops short of the ground floor, where full-height glazing optimizes engagement with the gardens. This use of rudimentary shapes persists elsewhere in the architecture, such as a moon window at the main staircase, and portals of wood and metal that frame vistas and shelter terraces. American architect Louis Kahn's circular cut-outs for the National Assembly Building in Dhaka, Bangladesh, were the inspiration, with simple forms that make an impact with their clarity.

To give character to the form, we chose cladding materials that loosely represent the different occupants. The adjacent pairing of raw, fair-faced concrete for the daughter's block and finished timber for the communal block results in a dialogue of incompleteness versus completeness. We also experimented with different ways of articulating the edges of the building for emphasis. An example is the gabled ends of the pitched-roof volumes. One omits a finishing layer of paint, so that the red primer for the aluminium frame accents the portal. Another encloses a screen of timber battens in an L-shaped stainless-steel bracket.

Timber is used liberally throughout the house to give it a strong tactility. When employed as screens, it filters the harsh sunlight and offers studies on how light behaves in and on the house. The most climactic expression is at the entrance foyer, where the interlocking of horizontal and vertical timber screens casts shadowed lattices. As these patterns shift and dance in response to the intensity and direction of the sunlight, they impress upon the occupants a strong sense of time and place.

SECTION

0   2   5        10m

The gym on the left, the main block and the daughter's block on the right enjoy views of the swimming pool.

Transparency in the bridges allows for appreciation of the house's diverse materiality (top and bottom). 179

180    Industrial and raw materials in the daughter's block exude a more youthful ambience.

GROUND FLOOR PLAN

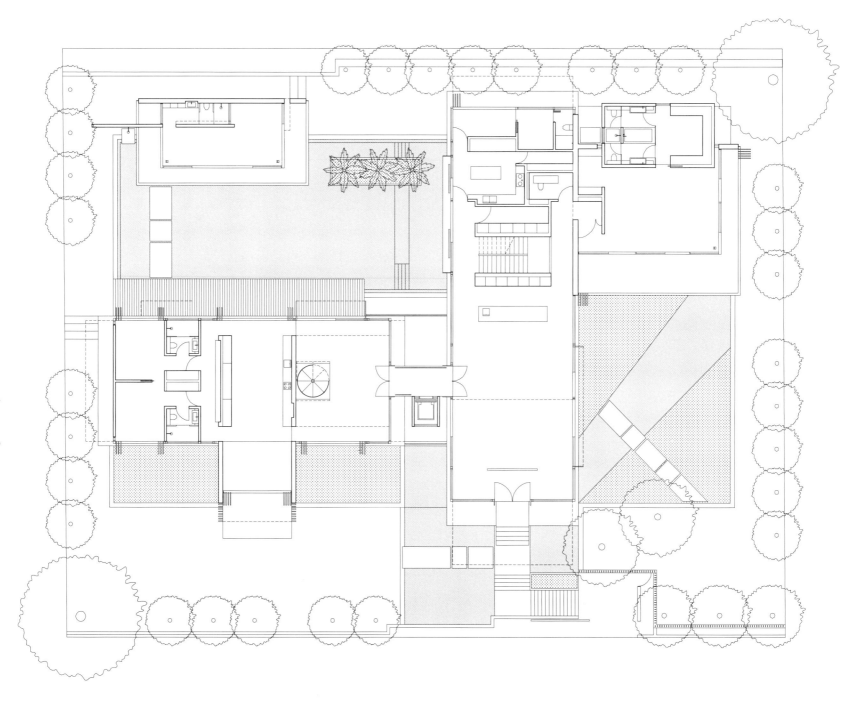

0  1  2          5m

FIRST FLOOR PLAN

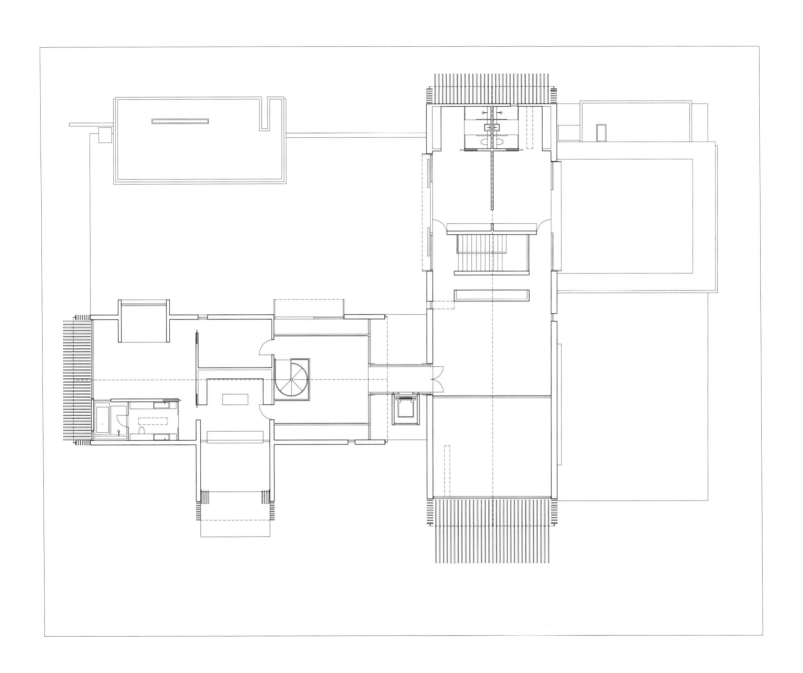

0   2   5   10m

184    Interlocking and layering elements create interesting shadows and spaces.

Screens, apertures and steel mesh balustrades further the discourse on shadows and shade (middle and above).  185

The client's bedroom overlooks a Zen garden at the rear.

The architecture explores different characters of cladding material.

# House with Slots

Vertical slots as a tropical device

Openings in the front elevation open up like flaps of boxes.

Rethinking the Tropical House    20 Years of RT+Q Architects

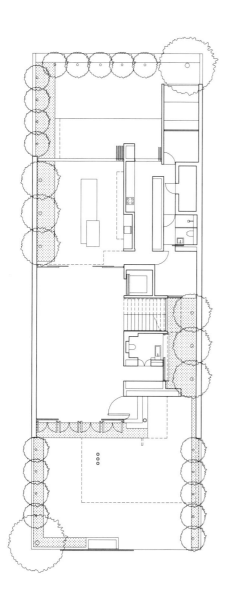

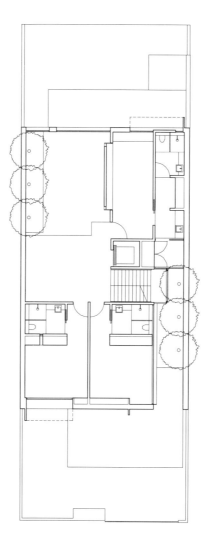

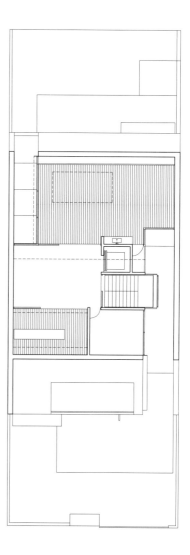

0  1  2        5n

It seems counterintuitive to give up precious square footage on a narrow plot to a non-functional use. But this planning makes sense if one considers the richness and delights of nature that abide in this void – sunlight, wind and engagement with nature's shifting rhythms through the day. In designing intermediate terraced houses, we often detach spaces from the party wall to create a sliver of an air well. The simple gesture immediately transforms shadowed interiors, which come about from being wedged on two sides by party walls, into a delightful and thermally comfortable dwelling.

The strategy is used in House with Slots to rejuvenate a plot that the semi-retired owners had lived in for thirty years. They had many fond memories of the original house but wanted an update to accommodate their love of nature, cooking and entertaining, as well as visits from their grown children and grandchildren. The main thesis of the house is 'slots', which take on manifold interpretations in both plan and tectonic expression. Our intention was to create a purposeful and neat architecture around a single theme.

Instead of a single air well abutting one party wall, as commonly found in terraced or semi-detached houses in Singapore, we inserted two 'slots'. The front slot tunnels alongside the staircase as well as a small multi-purpose room and guest bathroom on the ground floor before terminating at the centre of the plan. The second slot faces the rear garden along the opposite party wall. With no glass or wall segregating it from the double-volume dining and dry kitchen areas, this slot widens into an entire room of light. It segues with the rear garden through a two-storey glass wall to augment the pavilion-in-the-garden atmosphere. A wall of operable windows at the bottom layer allows for seamless indoor–outdoor access. The rear of the house embodies a strong semi-outdoor ambience. This originates from the owners' desire to have not only plants but also trees indoors, which steered the original discussions about positioning a water body at the slot into the idea of inserting a green lung.

We connected the ground- and first-floor internal spaces with a family room that overlooks the atrium and enjoys the vista of the rear garden beyond. At the edge of this space, a part of the floor plate extends outward like a Juliet balcony. It is articulated with a red steel plate, which interrupts the continuity of the glass balustrade. The same material is used as a centre wall-cum-handrail for the staircase. Its crisp profile matches the language of the canopies on the exterior.

The idea of 'slots' also manifests in the front and rear façades, where the canopies of openings unfold like gift-box flaps. The origami-like effect is enhanced by the distinct employment of materials and the thin profiles of the canopies. Their external surfaces are constructed from metal plates painted white to match the façade and the soffits, which are clad in composite timber. As a counterpoint to the predominantly white walls, the industrial, fair-faced concrete finish of the internal party wall was retained to visually enhance the detachment of the party wall from the autonomous house volume.

In the attic, we tapered the canopies on both front and back balconies upward to give a feeling of lightness to the architecture. This gesture changes the dynamic of the overall composition and accords it a playful character. The unfolding expressions on the façade repeat in the guest bathroom, with niches and walls distinguished with different types of marble as well as a washbasin designed as a protruding cuboid. Our aim was to create an artful, three-dimensional effect to bring delight to even utilitarian spaces.

SECTION

0    1    2        5m

192    The dining room opens to a lush rear garden (above); the rear 'slot' is integrated into the dining room as an internal garden (middle).

The guest bathroom opens to a linear courtyard.

194    The ceiling of the attic terrace 'flaps' open for more light (top); and a 'slot' of air and light at the house's rear (bottom).

The timber-clad ceiling of the attic terrace forms part of the interior experience.

# Modern Spirit, Classical Heart

—Lillian Tay

Director, VERITAS Architects, Malaysia

Forty years ago, I wrote a letter to a Rene Tan from Penang to convince him to enrol at Princeton, where I was in my freshman year. Rene went instead to Yale to study music and pursue his childhood dream of being a concert pianist. We found ourselves in the same Master's programme at Princeton a few years later. He laughed, said he injured a finger from relentless practice and settled for architecture.

In studio, Rene was no less relentless – a man possessed, sleep-deprived, with bloodshot eyes, oblivious to all around, immersed in a grand Rachmaninoff concerto with his prized collection of 300 classical music cassettes at his side. Bent over his drawing board in the infamous all-nighter studio, he would toil for many nights, churning out meticulous drawings, stopping only to tap to the beat of a beloved melody.

At final pin-up, Rene's intricately rendered pencil drawings would always overflow the walls of the studio with twice as many drawings as other students, including myself. He revelled in the geometry and order of classical architecture – pure forms in the manner of the innovative French neoclassical architect Claude-Nicolas Ledoux, often cast in the chiaroscuro and drama of a Piranesian landscape. That is how he won the heart of the stern Ralph Lerner, dean of Princeton's

architecture school, with whom he worked after graduation.

Rene's belief in classical forms and narrative from his architectural adolescence in the post-modern era is enriched by his equal passion for modern architecture and Le Corbusier. This was perhaps the influence of our tutor Alan Colquhoun, a renowned theorist on Le Corbusier who instilled an enduring belief in the clarity and rationality of the modern movement. Rene continued his immersion in Le Corbusier while teaching at Syracuse University in New York.

In 1996, Rene returned not to Malaysia but to Singapore, to join the newly formed SCDA Architects. He then ventured out in 2003 to form RT+Q Architects with TK Quek and continued his prolific journey, creating well over a hundred projects and evolving a clear signature. Gleaned from a continual revisiting and analysis of the forms and principles of modern architecture but also grounded in the purity of classical geometry, the style of the practice's works is disciplined yet playful, never without a mischievous narrative that delights in moments of surprise or subtle tributes to those Great Ones who came before.

TK has been a towering presence too, providing a strong guiding hand and grounding for the spirited explorations of the interns under their wing. The rite of passage of every intern – to build by hand a model of one of Le Corbusier's

projects – has created a complete library of models of the entire oeuvre of the Grand Master. This has become a unique and enthralling exhibition that is now travelling the world.

Twenty years on, RT+Q continues to develop its distinctive design identity, creating forms, spaces and meticulous details that are thoroughly modern in experience and, at the same time, celebrate and embed the geometric rigour of classical forms. Lastly, and it certainly must be said, the indefatigable team at RT+Q seems to relish every moment of its amazing journey.

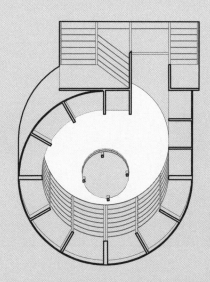

# Equilibrio Perfetto (Perfect Balance)

—Alexander Wong

Director and Founder, Alexander Wong Architects,
Hong Kong, China

As an architect and architectural writer, I sometimes fantasize about being someone like Giorgio Vasari living in an age of renaissance in Asia and writing about the most talented architects and inventors of our time, from the Leonardo to the Brunelleschi or the Michelangelo living among us all. And of course, one of those exceptional talents (some would say geniuses) we have in Singapore is none other than my close friend from Princeton – now the much revered architect of Southeast Asia, Rene Tan.

If Michelangelo is the benchmark against which to evaluate all subsequent geniuses (or genii), then his contributions to and mastery of sculpture, painting and architecture established the standards for many to emulate. With Rene's talents in classical music, sports and architecture, he has been a beacon for us all. But increasingly, as the years go by, I believe Rene has developed into a major educator in our professional discipline too. He has nurtured many dozens, if not hundreds, of budding talents at RT+Q Architects as well as those in the trenches of design studios at multiple universities – from Syracuse University in his early days to the National University of Singapore and Singapore University of Technology and Design today.

In the larger scheme of things, we are all here on this planet for only a very short period in time. However, architecture allows our imagination to travel beyond such limitations with the innocent belief that some ideas could almost become everlasting – no matter how briefly they seem to appear in this space-time continuum we call reality. I remember well my first encounter with Rene at Princeton (every other student was already talking about his incredible talents), when he happily rode into campus on his bicycle, wearing a scarf (from Yale?) and beaming with hope and vitality. It made such an impression on me without my knowing exactly why. Maybe it was because Albert Einstein, who happened to have lived in Princeton as well but in another era, also made himself famous by riding a bicycle in a publicity photograph, with an unforgettable quote to match: 'Life is like riding a bicycle. To keep your balance, you must keep moving.'

Rene has never lost his sense of balance or stopped moving forward towards greater endeavours and, dare we say, even more mind-blowing achievements. Perhaps only the future will fully tell us all.

The triangulated courtyards are both functional and dynamic in plan and section.

# Meshed Up House

Revisiting the plastic form in a terraced house

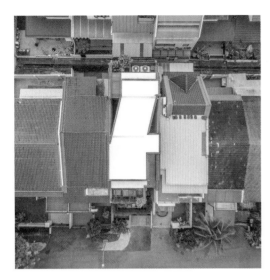

This project rethinks the terraced house typology, starting with a study on how to bring increased natural light and ventilation into a 25-metre-long (82-foot) plot that measures only 6.4 metres (21 feet) wide. It ended up being much more, including a study on lightness and the interplay of light and shadow. The house belongs to the firm's category of works that employ courtyards to open the interiors to the elements. It does this in a similar manner to an earlier project, the House at Watten (pp. 24–29), where a sculptural mass was inserted between the two party walls and the default negative spaces form the courtyards.

Here, the skewed massing results in two triangulated courtyards with skylights. The courtyards also allow rain, water and sunlight to penetrate into the house's innermost parts and create pleasant atmospheres for the family. The massing clearly reflects the functional layout where the main spaces, such as the living room, dining room and bedrooms, are housed in the double-bent volume, and the bathrooms and circulation spaces are located in three-storey boxes inserted within the courtyards. As this is a multigenerational household, privacy for each member was closely catered for. The courtyards that cut through the section of the house bridge these spaces in a vertical manner.

The goal of a porous house continues in the design of the spaces and the detailing. While the footprint of the house is not large, several lofty or 'great' spaces spread through the plan

Terraced House, Singapore 2015–2018

Spatial respites in the plan (top); the façade offers alternating encounters of transparency and translucency (above).

GROUND FLOOR PLAN        FIRST FLOOR PLAN        SECOND FLOOR PLAN        ATTIC PLAN

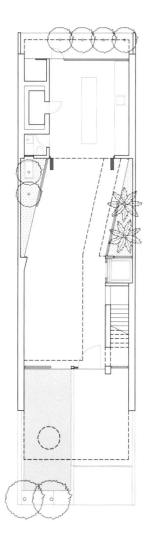
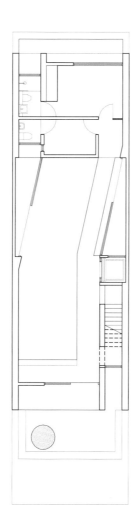
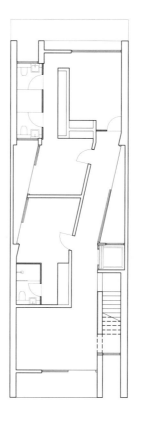
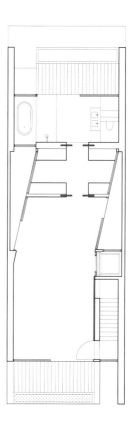

0  1  2     5m

imbue it with a spacious and airy character – a strategy we try to introduce to every project. One of them is the double-height living and dining area, brightened by natural light spilling in from the courtyard. A bridge cuts through this space, its sinewy shape reiterating the irregular plan. It leads from the study area at the front of the house to the grandmother's room and some utility spaces in the rear.

At the front of the house, the bridge expands vertically into a two-storey study area on a mezzanine that overlooks the living room. Sliding glass doors and screens create continuity between the study and a cosy, decked balcony lined with greenery that composes a part of the façade. The bridge, made of black steel plate and metal mesh, takes on an industrial nature. In the study, it becomes a single entity with a steel mesh bookshelf. Together, these homogeneous elements draw attention as a peculiar object suspended above the main communal areas.

Another strategy to bring light into the home is the use of transparent and translucent materials. A wall of glass blocks on the façade encloses the staircase for privacy while letting in diffused light. Screens that layer skylights and other large glass surfaces also filter harsh direct light. Metal mesh is employed not only at the bridge and study shelves, but throughout the house as a feature material – for instance, on cabinetry and on the main gate – hence the house's name. This material gives the house a casual character, which we complemented with several playful elements: a red metal mesh balcony, expressed as a projecting box in the stair core, and a mesh-encased oculus on the balcony that allows glimpses and light into the swimming pool below.

The contrast of tall and narrow spaces with alternating areas of light and shade offers a visceral experience when traversing the house. Such multitudinous textures and lively spaces frame the activities of family life within this smallish plot.

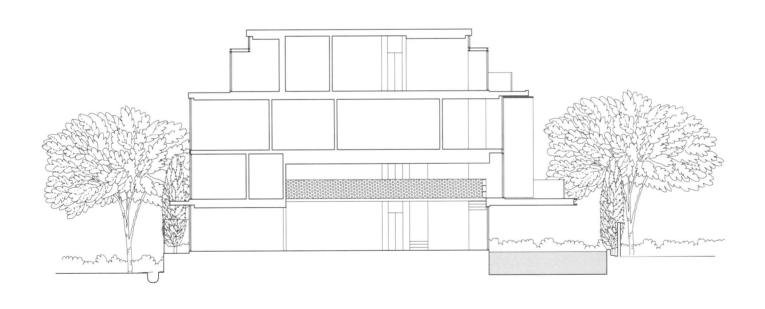

SECTION

0  1  2  5m

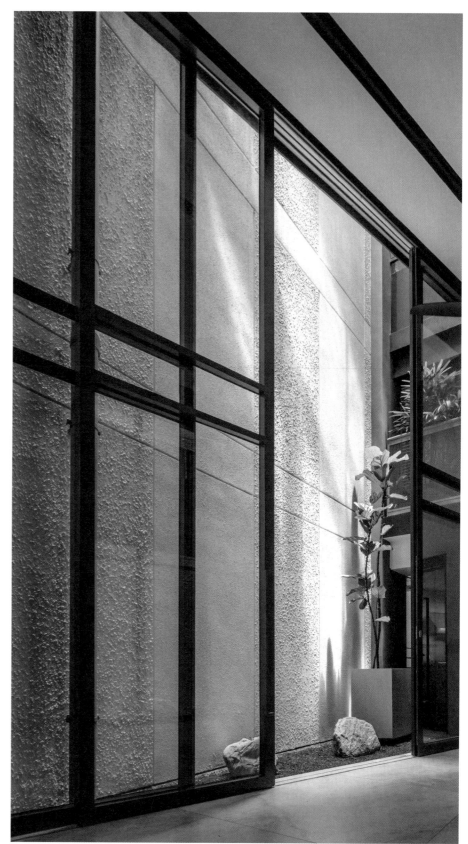

Double-height sliding glass doors maximize penetration of light and views inward (top left and above); alternative views from the bridge (bottom left).

The bridge is an eventful way of linking up spaces at the front and rear of the plot.

# House with a Sanctum

An antithetical approach to space, art and form

The myriad interventions to the exterior (above) contrast with the purity of the sanctum in the centre of the house (opposite).

SECTION

0  1  2      5m

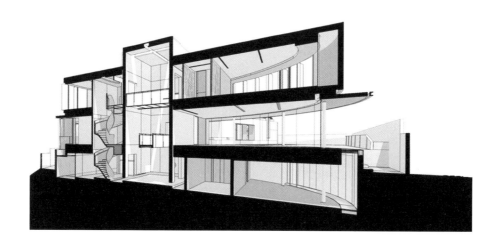

This house is an anomaly in our oeuvre. Unlike others that build upon the modernist box or vernacular, pitched-roof profile, it has an ovoid form. Yet it is not pure. Four linear protrusions emerging from the main body break our inclination for neatly contained volumes – a scheme guided by the client's brief for a non-ubiquitous house style. We decided this organic shape was the most suitable for the irregularly shaped plot. It allows the client – a keen horticulturist – to enjoy the landscaping in its entirety and in a fluid, ambulatory manner. This decision was sealed by our observation of her leanings towards curves in her art collection.

Conceptualized as a sculptural object in a garden, the house asserts its presence on the street but the soft lines mitigate its imposition on the streetscape. The 1,143-square-metre (12,300-square-foot) structure sits on a lushly planted 1,459-square-metre (15,700-square-foot) plot. Heeding Romanian sculptor Constantin Brancusi's view that 'architecture is inhabited sculpture', we carefully crafted each surface, space and trajectory. In the process, new discoveries of shaping and perceiving space were forged. The boxy protrusions accord privacy and more immersive enjoyment of specific pockets of the garden while remaining part of a larger whole. A pair on the ground floor are self-contained wings for family members, while another two on the first floor accommodate a pool and a terrace for the client to tend to her favourite potted plants.

The formal entry sequence begins up a flight of steps towards a circular window. This perfect circle, inspired by moon gates in Chinese gardens, is one of the many ways we attempt to engage the interiors with the external environment. In another instance, we peeled the skin of the façade slightly to introduce indirect light into the house. Similar intentions shaped the tectonic projections, including the cantilevered blocks encased in laser-cut aluminium panels, a small window with a crimson aluminium frame, and a red steel washbasin counter-cum-planter in the guest bathroom that extends out of the house's skin to blur object and architecture. They upend the conventional scale and readability of the domestic trope with a sense of playfulness and optimism.

Similarly, the varied geometric interventions make familial routines more interesting. The most dynamic is the living room's 180-degree curved glazing that presents a seamless panorama of nature, as well as a 12-metre-high (39-foot) void, or atrium, rising up the house's core. The latter 'sanctum' gives the dwelling its name and connects the basement to the upper floors. From the basement, the atrium's walls are slightly elevated with a band of glass at the base, providing intrigue as one enters the house. This also helps to brighten the underground corridors. A cruciform skylight inspired by Japanese architect Tadao Ando's Church of Light illuminates the atrium, which is interrupted by two criss-crossing paths bridging spaces across the plan. Although it was originally intended for displaying art, the client decided to keep the cube unadorned so that architecture and space in their purest forms can be enjoyed as an orchestration of light, air and enclosure.

As we did the façade, we jolted the purity of this metaphysical volume with doses of colour, seen in the bridges' blue-green glass floors and a scarlet peephole. Along with marble or stone, paint is also a material that affects emotions and gives focus to elements. Carmine colours the inside of an outdoor spiral staircase connecting garden and pool, as well as the basement's elliptical guest bathroom; a turquoise skylight mirrors the shade of the sky as one ascends from basement to ground floor. We selected the hues based on Le Corbusier's architectural polychromatic colour keyboards developed between 1931 and 1959, choosing punchier shades to contrast with the house's grey palette.

Between the ground and the first floor, we inserted a slim, 1-metre (3⅓-foot) overhang that provides shelter and softens the house's bulk. The building's structure prioritizes formal clarity. For example, the floors of the cantilevering protrusions were raised and extended to read as if they emerge out of the principal elliptical form as separate entities. To keep the pool structure visually light, the massive beams are set in from the cantilevered sides and the loading is brought to the ground with a V-shaped column.

This project's amalgamation of parts appears complex at first, but it adheres to our core values of clear form, counterintuition and compositional harmony. It explores the rich possibilities of an architecture freed from archetypes but still guided by site and the programme of the unique brief and spatial requirements. In our studies on architectural theory, we have gleaned from Robert Venturi how architecture can be paradoxically richer and more interesting by creating ambiguous relationships and 'putting the right thing in the wrong place'. House with a Sanctum furthers our exploration of these thoughts.

Mechanical devices are celebrated rather than concealed.

The house's ovoid form allows the client to enjoy the enveloping foliage in its entirety.

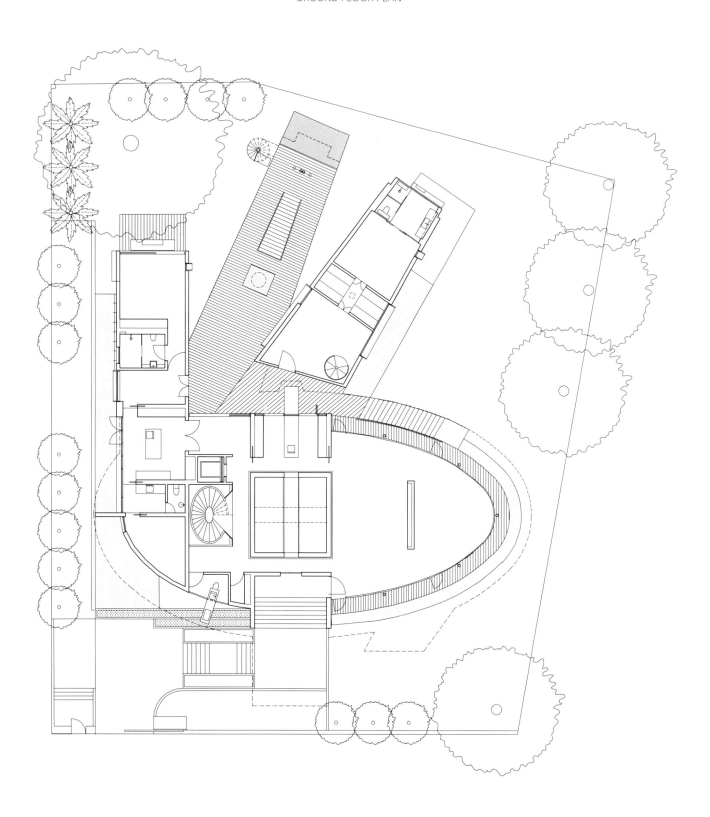

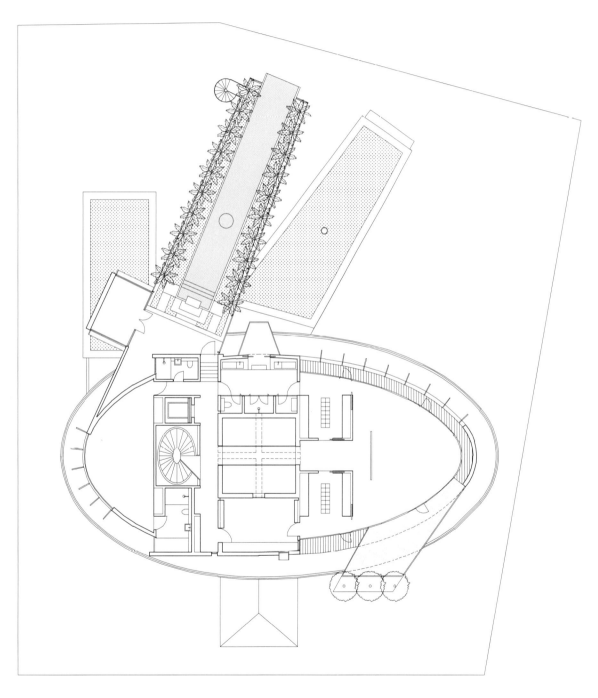

0  1  2        5m

212   'Fingers' protrude from the main oval, engaging with the garden at the guest bathroom (above), master bedroom (middle) and guest wing (opposite) respectively.

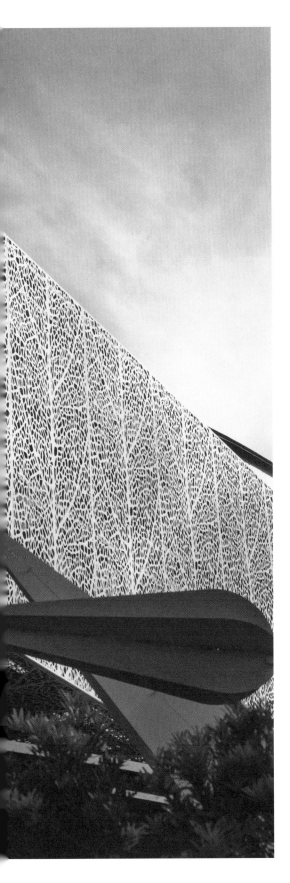

214   View looking up to the atrium (above); bridges in the atrium ritualize the circulation process (middle).

Views to adjacent spaces of the atrium are afforded through playful means.

216    The guest bathroom's washbasin as an internal and external object (above); chromatic experiments from the basement to the ground floor (middle).

Mesh skins at the pool (top) and basement access (bottom) perpetuate porosity.

# House with a Roof

A renewed investigation into the tropical roof

A belvedere edging the first-floor spaces allows the inhabitants to engage with nature.

The gym block is expressed as a cantilevering, autonomous object.

Located in a tree conservation area, this house is surrounded by mature trees and luxuriant greenery, and enjoys a view of rolling hills and a forest at the rear, which also buffers it from a school. Although the property was built for sale, the client understood the importance of a house that sensitively responds to this environment. Our scheme nestles it in its green context to unite shelter with land. While spaces were sited and oriented to take advantage of the undulating terrain and existing greenery, the general symmetry of the house's tectonics, spatial planning and façade composition creates a quiet, gentle presence.

In response to the wide street frontage, we positioned a long linear block at the front that is capped by a commanding large-span roof. The architectonics is clear and simple but strong, with a form reminiscent of the horizon. The house is sited on the higher part of the sloping land, which dips towards the rear and offers myriad encounters. Part of it is sunken, while the other perches aloft like a promontory, affording panoramic views at certain vantage points.

The massing is divided into three rectilinear blocks. The linear block upfront is followed by a second block that extends perpendicularly at the rear over the swimming pool. Seemingly floating off the water is a third guest block conceived as an autonomous pavilion. Its skewed arrangement throws a spanner into the composed layout. The open terrace space and a lap pool tie the three blocks together.

To ensure that nature is omnipresent throughout, each block features operable full-height glass that enables the house to breathe passively through natural and cross-ventilation. The natural scenery also ensures a sense of quietude and calm as one moves through. Some details were designed to enhance a feeling of unity with the environment. For instance, the bathroom in the guest wing opens to a view of trees that rise from lower ground, with a steel grating window, timber screens and a skylight. In contrast, another bathroom is fully enclosed and features a circular form that is counterintuitive to the general orthogonal direction. While there are other playful details – such as a floating basin, a full-height movable mirror and a paper holder made with slim black metal elements – the contemplative mood of the house remains.

For the bones of the house, we employed a hybrid steel and concrete structure. The main roof over the front linear block is constructed of steel trusses with a standing seam aluminium roof. Aluminium panels cladding the underside evoke the appearance of a monolithic object. The roof tapers at the top and bottom to achieve a slim edge detail on all four sides to lighten its look. Likewise for the overhanging eaves in the other two blocks that also provide shade. In the front linear block, a row of clerestory windows beneath the roof gives the impression that it is floating. This element is part of a layered composition on the façade, which starts with a solid base with timber cladding on the first floor. The two are joined by a trim of planters that lines the balcony. The overall serene composition is interspersed with slots and portals as elements of surprise and to give a sense of scale to the large surfaces – something that is a consistent strategy in our practice.

Visitors are welcomed into the reception foyer with a spiral staircase that is encased in a glass box like a gallery. Its central placement provides a strong symmetrical reading to the façade composition of the front block, while its organic lines encourage visitors to explore the house. Coated in white paint, the sculptural staircase brings the user through the subterranean bedrooms and up to the structured living spaces. Finally, one arrives at the belvedere, enclosed in clear glass, for an unencumbered view of nature.

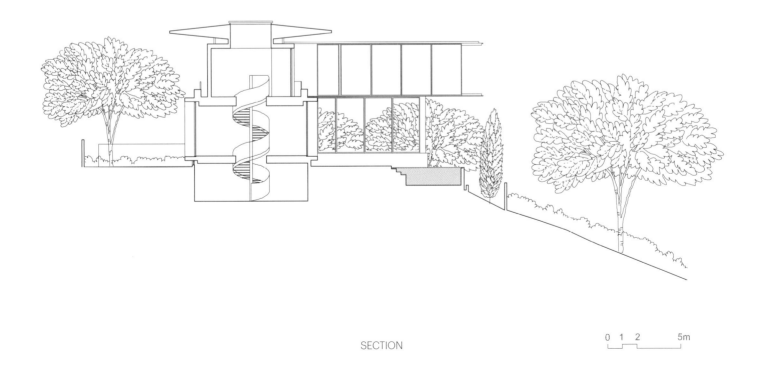

SECTION

0  1  2      5m

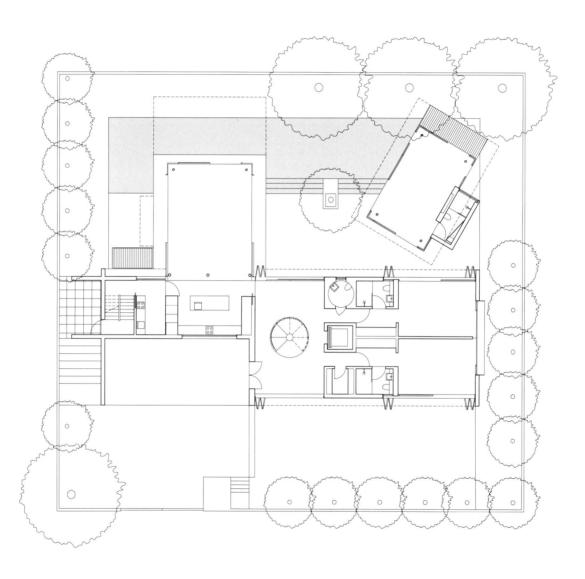

FIRST FLOOR PLAN

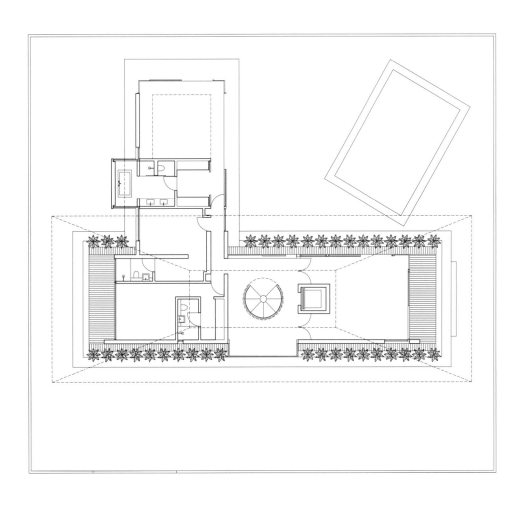

0 1 2        5m

224    The master bedroom cantilevers above the pool, enveloped by nature.

Borrowed green views enter the master bathroom.

226    Access between spaces is designed as strong, tactile experiences (above and opposite).

# House with Two Faces

In contrast to the closed-up front (middle), the rear opens up for views and light (above and opposite).

GROUND FLOOR PLAN

FIRST FLOOR PLAN

SECOND FLOOR PLAN

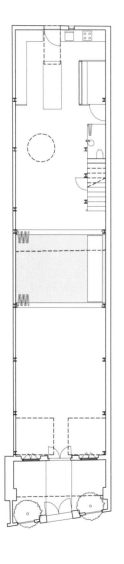

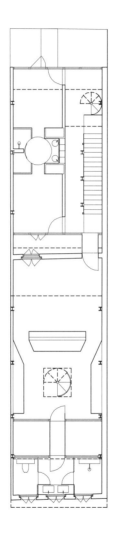

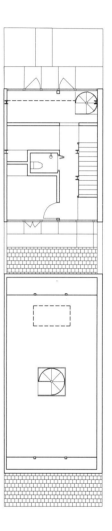

0  1  2      5m

This house's eccentric name alludes to its dual façade, addressing the dichotomies of old and new, mass and skin, heavy and light. The unique site, with the front facing a busy road and the rear opening to a quiet back lane, presented an opportunity for dual frontage that we gladly took. The shophouse is not slated for conservation but we recognized its architectural heritage and historical urban value, and sought to preserve it.

The beauty and dignity of the shophouse front is retained, including details such as timber-shuttered windows, decorative sashes and architraves. At the rear, an existing one-storey service area was demolished and replaced with a new, modern block wrapped in fritted glass and steel as a counterpoint to the historical front elevation. Instead of closing it up, this rear elevation is given importance in the back lane with a strong tectonic quality and transparency. While partly a response to urban setback guidelines, the staggered profile also animates the rear façade. The scale of the addition is carefully proportioned to mitigate the massing's impact on the urban skyline. The choice of modern construction materials gives it a disposition of lightness, and the generous use of glass washes natural light into the deep plot during the day. At night, the house illuminates the back lane with a warm glow akin to an urban lantern or street theatre.

Many elements within the house's modest footprint rethink the approach to shophouse intervention. In a contrarian move, we positioned the master bathroom at the front of the house. This buffers the master bedroom and walk-in wardrobe from the road noise while allowing it to be naturally ventilated. The access to the master bathroom is designed to be a highlight in the interior architecture. Above the foyer, a gap is cut through the first-floor floor slab to create a double-storey atrium where a bridge links the master bathroom and walk-in wardrobe across the void. It is a piece of floating artwork among the owner's other pieces of art in his vast collection, turning a nondescript moment into an event. Deep red paint applied to the steel elements of the bridge and the master bathroom's internal façade further give the space emphasis and character.

The red colour continues as a theme across the other parts of the house, such as at the entrance ceiling to the master bedroom and the juncture of the main staircase's steel structure. This celebrates the act of construction and reflects our tongue-in-cheek attitude to exposing rather than hiding the bones of the house, which we believe can be done in interesting and uplifting ways. The steel columns and beams that hold up the new concrete floor of the first floor above the living room are also exposed and

surgically nested into the old structure. In another instance, we exposed the floor of the bridge adjoining the master walk-in wardrobe and master bathroom, as well as the ceiling above the void. Both are made of a composite slab system of steel decking and concrete.

The result is an industrial aesthetic that is carried on through the house in elements such as lighting incorporated into the I-beam columns, corrugated metal panelling for walls in the dining room, as well as customized steel shelves in the

The round cut-out in the attic study room.

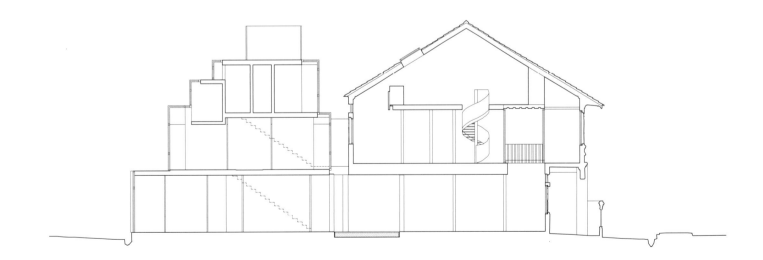

0  1  2          5m

232    Voids and glass walls engage the interior with the environment (above); an artwork of a Chinese migrant worker reflects the era the shophouse was built in (middle).

bathrooms. Between the old and new blocks on the ground floor, a void is left to become a water courtyard. This fulfilled the owner's request for a calm body of water within this entertainment zone, and also brings into the home intimate elements of tropical living through a gap in the roof as rainwater falls into the pond and breezes pass through to ventilate the home.

On the first floor, a spiral staircase offers an alternative quick access to the attic, which houses the maid's quarters and a sheltered terrace overlooking the back lane. The staircase design optimizes the house's small footprint and becomes a focal point in the space. It is mirrored in the original block with another white spiral staircase tunnelling from the master walk-in wardrobe to the attic, where the study and prayer room receive ample daytime illumination from a skylight. In keeping with our desire to tailor solutions, this spiral staircase is detailed as a piece of cabinetry, with slots in the structure for the owner's wife to display her shoes and handbags.

Throughout the house, we exposed some elements of the historical architecture such as original timber battens and parts of brick walls, the latter framed as features within plaster cutouts. By layering and expressing the old and new components clearly and deliberately, an authentic narrative and subplots unfold as one traverses the house.

Spiral staircases as sculpture (top) and storage in the walk-in wardrobe (bottom).

234    The industrial quality of the exposed bridge and ceiling lends interest to the plaster-and-paint shell (above and opposite).

The master bathroom is placed counterintuitively at the front of the house.

# House with Twin Gardens

A thesis on passive sustainability in the tropics

Large eaves, walls, fins and the placement of the main vertical access upfront all help to buffer the western sun (above and opposite).

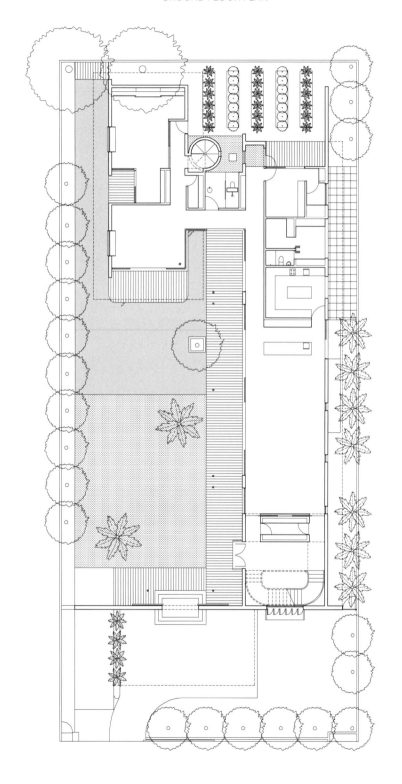

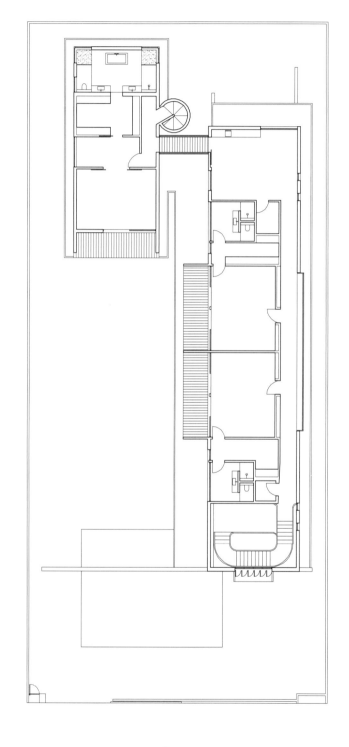

Rethinking the Tropical House   20 Years of RT+Q Architects

0    2    5              10m

The west-facing site of this house birthed a thesis on addressing the daily effects of the tropical climate without relying too much on mechanical means. Our overall objective was to craft a sustainable house, and key devices included the use of screening elements and the strategic organization of spaces to counter the discomforts of heat and glare. Beyond the main gate, a long wall lends the house an inward-looking demeanour. This is buffered by tall and lush planting upfront. A moon gate carved into the wall opens into a garden. Originating in Oriental gardens, this artistic device of framing and layering creates a nuanced way of moving through space and landscapes. A 25-metre (82-foot) lap pool runs along the edge of this garden towards the rear.

We begin the house's sequence with the grand gesture of a triple-storey foyer as the first spatial encounter within the house. It contains a sculptural staircase pulled sideways to fill the width of the space and to serve as a volumetric buffer between the façade and the living spaces. This strategy of setting the inner sanctums away from the street tackles issues of privacy and solar heat gain. The long front wall also allows the house to open freely into the courtyard and its landscaping at all times of the day without curtains or screens, as there is no need to worry about passers-by looking in. The entrance of the house is protected by wide overhanging eaves, a feature that is deployed consistently throughout, including along the spaces facing the garden to form a sheltered corridor. Together with full-height sliding partitions, it also allows for the house to be fully breathable in both rainy and sunny weather.

The spaces are housed in a simple L-shaped block that forms a courtyard around the front garden. The main living areas are housed in the front portion, with two bedrooms above. The rear arm contains a more private wing, with the family room and study on the ground floor, and the master bedroom above. The two levels are joined by a small spiral staircase that is articulated as a totemic structure cleaving to the exterior of the main building. Unlike the front staircase, which has an open nature, this one has a solid form, with small windows lending a monastic feel to the interior – inspired by a staircase in the Convent of La Tourette designed by Le Corbusier.

In the basement, we cut voids into the section to overcome the challenge of bringing natural light and air into the sunken space. A gap between the pool and front garden functions as an impluvium (a rainwater-catchment pool system in the Greco-Roman era), introducing sunlight and rain into the basement garage. The front staircase also serves as an air well from the basement to the first-floor ceiling, where a skylight illuminates the lower floor.

The relatively modest footprint of the house called for creative landscaping. The idea of twin gardens came out of a collaboration with the clients. While both offer greenery and outdoor spaces to enjoy, each embodies different functions and characters. The front garden is a lush tropical courtyard with undulating terrain, dotted with palm trees to foster a relaxed mood. The second garden, located at the back of the house, is where the study and the guest bedroom face. This is designed as an edible garden, where organic food is farmed and waste composted as a sustainable facet of modern living.

Within the rational organization, construction and architecture of the house, we inserted elements of surprise. A vaulted ceiling in the living room introduces a sense of spatial richness echoing Rococo architecture, while a single column in the basement painted sunflower yellow takes a page from Le Corbusier's use of colour in the Convent of La Tourette. These touches follow our mantra of putting the right thing in the wrong place, enlivening the repetitiveness of domestic events while functioning as spatial markers.

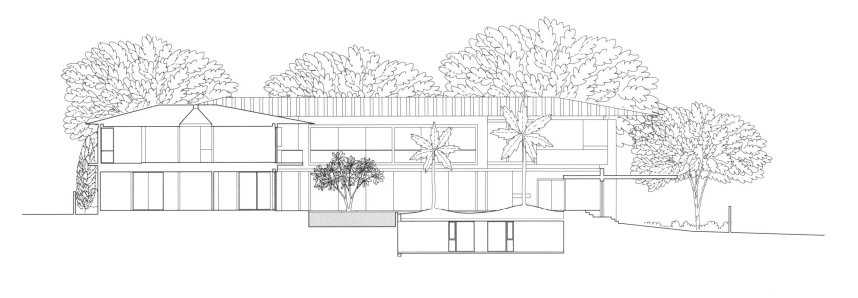

SECTION

0   2   5   10m

242    Staircases provide opportunities to create intrigue (above and above right).

A language of layering and framing enhances the entry sequence.

An undulating landscape facilitates the spilling out of activities to the garden.

Detail of timber integrated into steel columns.

The wide corridor buffers the main living areas from the heat and glare.

In the rear garden, organic crops are grown for consumption and recycled, for sustainable modern living.

# House with Gables Form as remembrance

The house is a thesis on the gabled roof form, which presents a gentle front to the street.

Celebration of light and space in the double-height foyer (above); rafters accentuate the height of the family room (top); detailing of a dormer window (bottom).

The design of this house is guided by a sentiment for the past but is not beholden to it. Instead, the elements of an existing house on the plot became a driver for an exercise in geometric clarity and formal poetry, where the essence of the old is modernized through clean lines. The client had lived with her family in the home for thirty years and had forged many treasured memories. Now that her son and daughter are adults and needed more space of their own (the son lives here with his young family), the matriarch wanted to rebuild the house to cater to their future needs.

The entrance level of the old house dipped lower than the main road. This gave privacy, but its position on the plot presented some inconveniences. It was located at the end of the driveway, which made manoeuvring and parking cars a constant annoyance. We pushed the new house nearer to the entrance and reoriented it parallel to the driveway. Four parking slots now nestle neatly under the building, improving the driveway's functionality.

The house's new orientation preserves the land's natural slope. We took advantage of the level differences with a spatial layout of dramatic play. The foyer, living room and garden are arranged sequentially in three tiers over a 5-metre (16-foot) difference from the front to the rear of the site, generating panoramic sightlines. The strategy of not over-building and of pushing the house towards the front of the plot turned the rear garden into a 13-metre-long (42½-foot), flat space ideal for the grandchild to run about in. Such visual and physical layering emphasizes the theme of connectivity and fluidity of spaces.

The massing of the house is a direct correlation to the multigenerational programming. Two blocks stretch towards the garden, each a self-contained unit with a kitchenette and a family room. The matriarch's suite physically and symbolically joins the two at the centre. As the family was fond of the old house's gabled form, this became the governing scheme of the new house. The roof plan organizes the spaces on the first floor. It bears down on the ground floor, where exaggerated eaves shade 6-metre-deep (20-foot) verandas, and slim pilotis maintain the purity and lightness of these protrusions. The expansive verandas encourage ventilation and airflow into the internal spaces, promoting comfortable outdoor living over air-conditioned rooms. The provision of such generous tropical spaces makes the house sustainable.

The foyer affords further visual and sensorial spectacle. The space ascends all the way to the underside of the gabled roof. Articulated rafters

Details tie the scale and composition together at the roof (above left), foyer staircase (middle) and guest bathroom (above right).

Metal edge details emphasize the forms of the roof and dormer windows.

pay homage to similar ones in the old house but are painted white as a contemporised manifestation of the past. A patterning of vertical and horizontal lines also breaks the perception of the ceiling expanse. We tucked the vertical circulation to the sides – lift shaft on the left and staircase to the right – to allow for an unblocked view in the centre from the main entrance to the garden. Just like in the old house, twin dormer windows infuse the foyer with skyward views and light, as in a chapel. The double-height space also creates a stack effect that encourages ventilation. This uplifting effect repeats in the family rooms of the children's wings, albeit in a more extroverted sense, with screened elevations offering garden views. Each wing's ceilings are also given character, with a vaulted foyer on the daughter's side and a flat cove design for the son's suite.

The muted palette of simple materials results in a neutral backdrop for assimilating the existing furniture and fittings that hold sentimental value for the clients. While the architecture of the house is far from avant-garde, its beauty lies in its concise focus on the elemental effects of pure space, pure form and pure light.

An aperture in the garden wall.

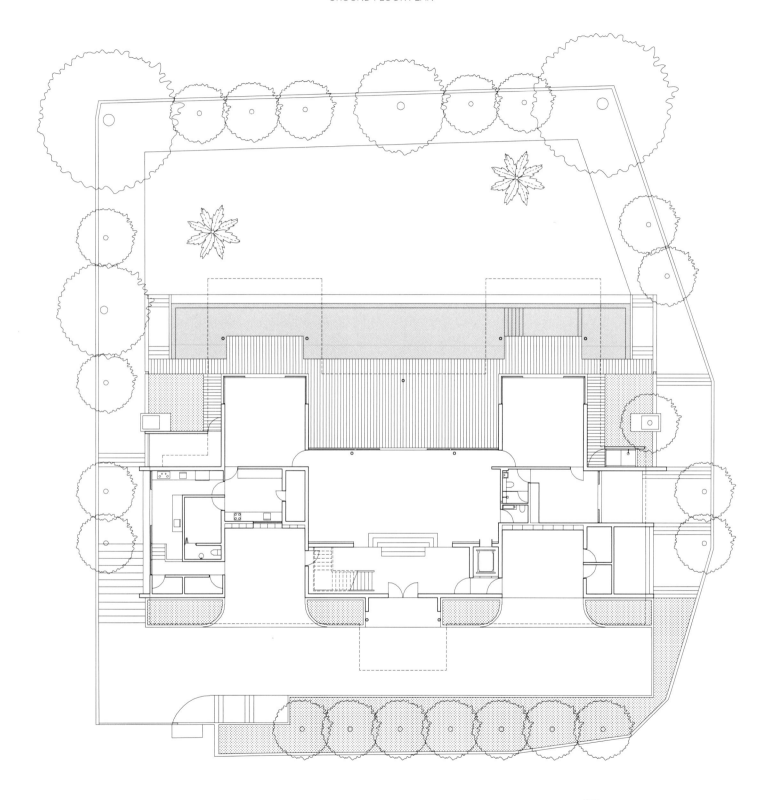

Rethinking the Tropical House    20 Years of RT+Q Architects

0 1 2    5m

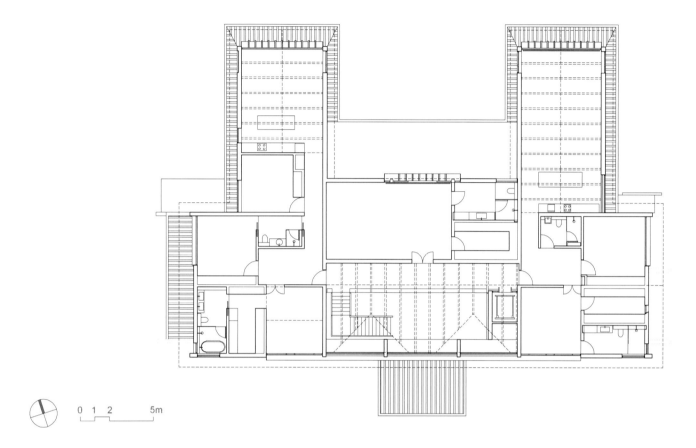

0 1 2    5m

SECTION

0 1 2    5m

256    A fluid unfolding of spaces from the foyer to the open terrace and pool traces the undulating terrain.

Six-metre-long (20-foot) canopies facing the rear garden create usable, sheltered spaces.

# House with an Oculus
Adapting the Roman oculus for the tropics

This project rethinks how to illuminate a house through the use of vertical apertures. The theme came about because of the site's challenging topography. Developed for sale, the house sits on a site located on a steep slope, with an underground train tunnel running beneath it and three large tembusu trees at the rear that had to be retained. Tasked with building a good-sized house that would appeal to a broad spectrum of tastes and make the best of its unique topography, we sought to retain the sloped terrain as landscape in a section-driven scheme while devising different ways of bringing natural light and ventilation into the basement level.

The main living areas were placed on higher ground to take advantage of the site, which is raised 5 metres (16 feet) above the road, offering elevated views towards the city. Beneath sits the basement, which opens to the road and is tucked into the earth. While most excavated basements make do with minimal ceiling heights, we were able to give this space a 4-metre-high (13-foot) ceiling thanks to the steep topography. On the elevated ground floor, the architectural parti

(key concept diagram) reads as two parallel two-storey blocks joined by a circulation core facing a garden and swimming pool. The need for significant structural support for the ground-floor outdoor spaces presented an opportunity to design a funnel-shaped column in the basement driveway that makes a statement to visitors on arrival.

Every opportunity was taken to vertically connect the basement to the upper levels in order to facilitate communication within the household and to brighten the space. One example is a narrow light court carved from a side garden to bring daylight into the entertainment room in the basement. Another is an oculus topped with a skylight that connects all three floors from the entrance foyer at the basement up to the staircase landing of the first floor. It sits at the connecting portion between the two parallel blocks and becomes the heart of our scheme. The family who bought the house discovered that the oculus also worked as a convenient loudspeaker to gather everyone for meals in the dining room on the ground floor. As in ancient times, the oculus also functions as a sundial, alerting one to the different times of the day. Similar encounters occur in the guest bathroom and the walk-in wardrobe in the master bedroom, where smaller oculi bring light into these spaces with few or no windows.

Apart from the central oculus, we clad the lift shaft in glass and the staircase in timber screens to enhance the vertical flow of light and air from outside. Movable teak screens define the exterior of the first floor to control the modulation of shade, heat and privacy to the six bedrooms. The hip roof also extends far beyond the building's edge lines to create a tropically responsive architecture. The ends of the roof are lightened with an aluminium trellis fin, while timber-clad undersides unite it with other elements of the same material, such as sliding door frames, internal and external wall cladding, and the brise-soleil. Such use of natural materials integrates the house with the garden and the backdrop of towering tembusu trees visually and in a tactile manner. This is further enhanced by the walls of natural slate and timber-textured fair-faced concrete, including in the basement, where it lends a cavernous quality in contrast with the lightness of the architecture above.

A central oculus topped with a skylight connects from the basement to the first-floor staircase landing.

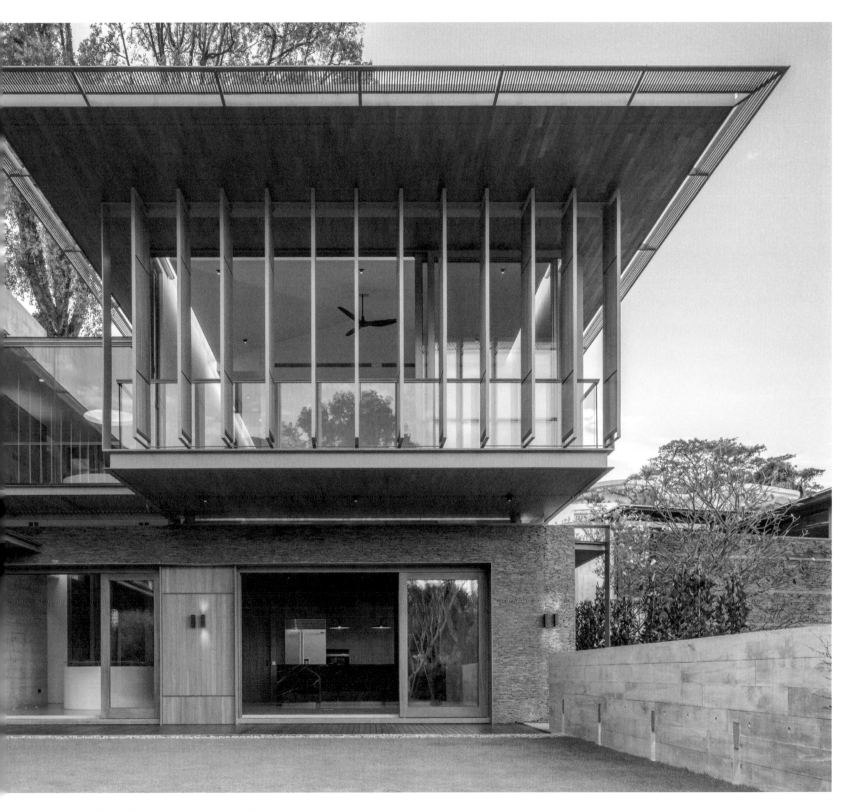

Expansive roofs reinforce the house's tropicality.

262    The steep topography allowed for a 4-metre-high (13-foot) basement entrance.

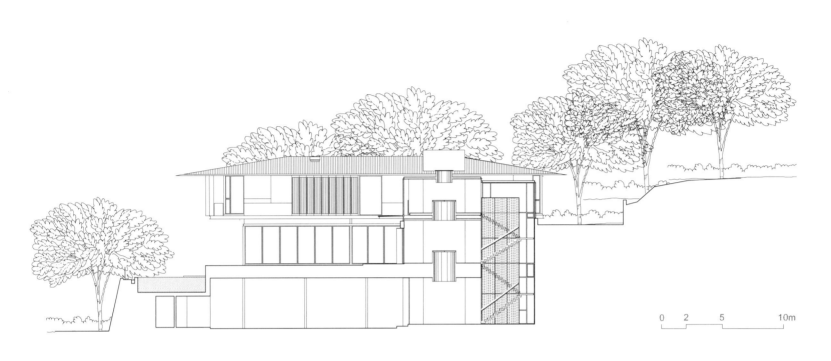

0 2 5 10m

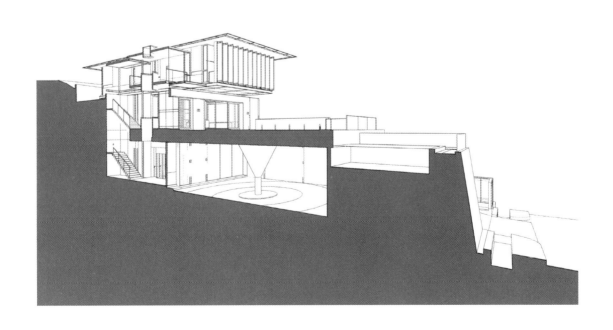

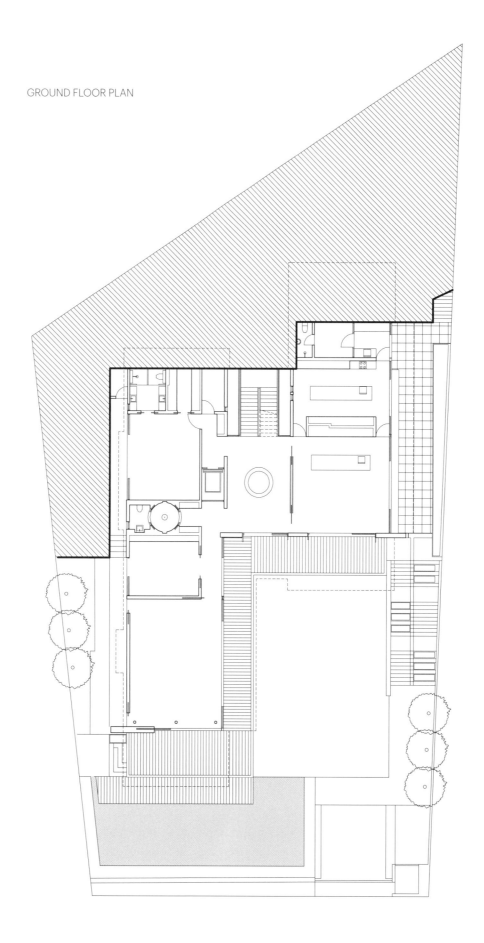

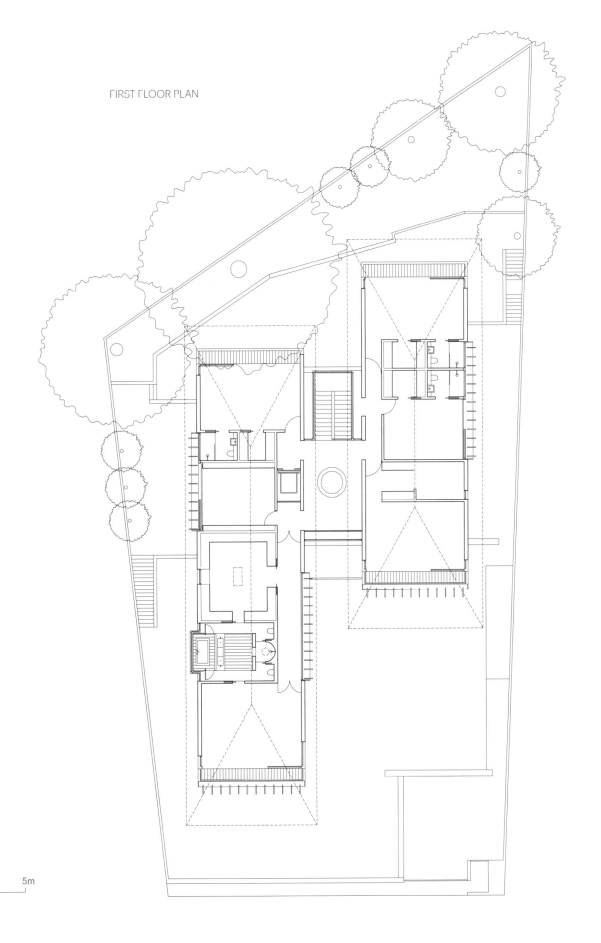

FIRST FLOOR PLAN

House with an Oculus

0  1  2        5m

266    The oculus is a modern adaptation of a classical spatial technique (bottom).

Teak cladding on interior and exterior surfaces harmonizes the house with nature (opposite top and above).

# Petit Jervois

A reimagining of the compact apartment

The architecture offers a sleek counterpoint to the architecturally busy neighbourhood.

Pedestrian bridge above car ramp (top); leitmotif of cubic forms (bottom).    269

This is the first of a new range of 'compact luxury' apartments in the city conceptualized with the client to address modern-day living demands. We believe that size should not compromise quality, but instead provide opportunities for architectural innovation and refinement. To differentiate this property from the client's more conventional apartments, we leaned towards a raw foundry-like aesthetic, which celebrates the art of craftsmanship and detailing of materials. Minimal surface treatment is applied to textures, structure and finishes to retain their natural states as much as possible. A base palette of cool, neutral tones is enlivened with warm lighting and accent elements.

Likewise, the architecture is clean, clear and strong, guided by modernist and classical principles of form and space planning within a site of multiple constraints. The irregular trapezoidal site is bounded by large drainage reserves along three of its four sides. By optimizing rather than maximizing, our scheme places equal importance on public spaces and private dwellings. Some fifty-five units are distributed between a pair of five-storey cubes, whose geometric purity was inspired by Le Corbusier's 'Lesson of Rome'. His writings champion the use of unadulterated geometric shapes to express the 'pure and simple beauty of architecture', as well as to bring purpose and order to the chaos of nature, which in this case also refers to the irregularity of the plot.

The genesis of the architectural diagram stems from a conventional rectangular slab-block massing cut into half, detached and swung 90 degrees. Compared to a single rectilinear block, this resolution offers more elevations and, correspondingly, more natural light and views. It also results in two courtyards – a more public court containing the driveway and a private one with the swimming pool in the rear as a tranquil oasis for residents. These courts, as well as the peripheral areas, are lushly landscaped like French gardens, in which the residents can enjoy strolling despite the petite site. We also looked to nature in the detailing of the two blocks. Resembling a piece of geode split open to reveal its crystal within, the two inner elevations facing the driveway are clad in full-height, unobstructed, smooth curtain wall glass, while the outer elevations feature a skin of steel frames and aluminium sun-shading fins.

This dual expression is also contextual. The curtain walls bring natural light from the cooler

morning sun into the units facing the vehicular drop-off canopies, while the rear façades have sliding glass doors opening on to balconies that enable residents to enjoy outdoor living and views of the private pool oasis. The depth of the balconies creates a semi-outdoor volumetric buffer zone to protect internal spaces from the harsh western sun. The aluminium fins serve as additional shields, placed at strategic angles to provide some privacy between units while maintaining the pool views.

In congruence with the architecture, the development is assiduously detailed, with cube-like elements on both macro and micro scales. For instance, each block's vehicular drop-off canopy is expressed as a cuboid finished in reddish-brown panels to distinguish them as entry portals. Gridded metal screens clad the guardhouse and a small gym by the pool, and are also adopted to conceal services in the common corridors. Together with the off-form concrete walls and exposed steel beams employed in other parts of the common areas, this industrial aesthetic is a counterpoint to the development's otherwise refined sensibilities.

The layout pays homage to another modernist architect, Ludwig Mies van der Rohe. His design for the Farnsworth House, an apotheosis of 20th-century modern living, positioned the main spaces around a central core. Similarly in this development, the lifts, staircases and service risers were located within the centre of the floor plate, leaving the perimeter for units. On a unit scale, the bathrooms are centralized within the plan, thus freeing the edges for residents to enjoy and control the extent of natural ventilation, light and views. The bathrooms are expressed as timber boxes in line with the cube leitmotif.

With this layout, the apartments enjoy flexibility and adaptability despite their size. The interiors were conceptualized as spaces rather than rooms, and can be combined or divided with large-format, movable partitions according to preference. At the same time, we were adamant that the apartments, while small, should enjoy simple functional luxuries in the form of customized elements. Examples are hooks integrated into unit number plates for delivery services, customized faceplates for switches and sockets, and trays in the bathrooms for toiletries, reading materials or mobile phones. Every detail points to our goal of offering livable, versatile and resilient homes in the context of modern and sustainable 'downsized' living in the tropics.

SECTION

0 2 5 10m

Petit Jervois

The gym is presented as a neat cube (top); a detail of the screen façade (bottom).

Dense hedges and trees with spreading canopies function as shields and buffers between communal and private living areas.

Petit Jervois

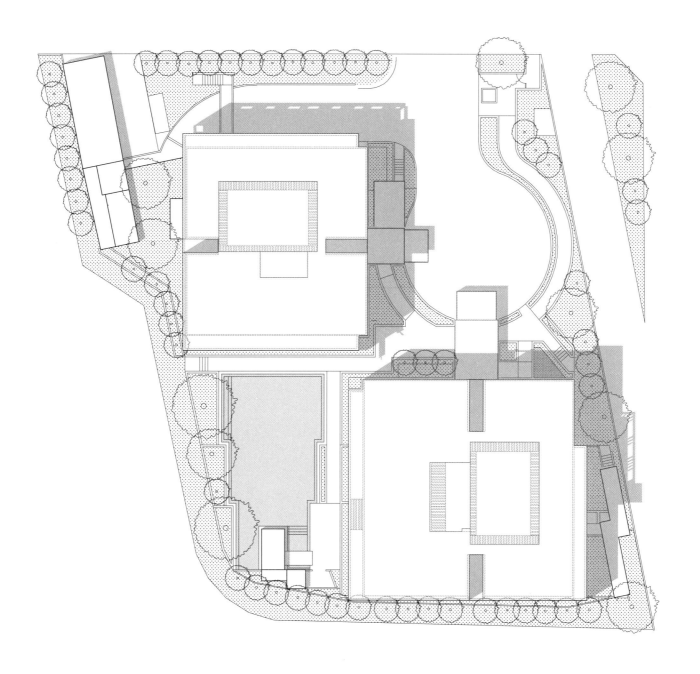

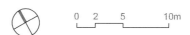

The driveway's location at the front of the plot gives the blocks privacy from the street.

276    Basement lift lobby with Rene's paintings (top left); bedroom (top right); entrance lobby (bottom left); bathroom expressed as an autonomous unit (bottom right).

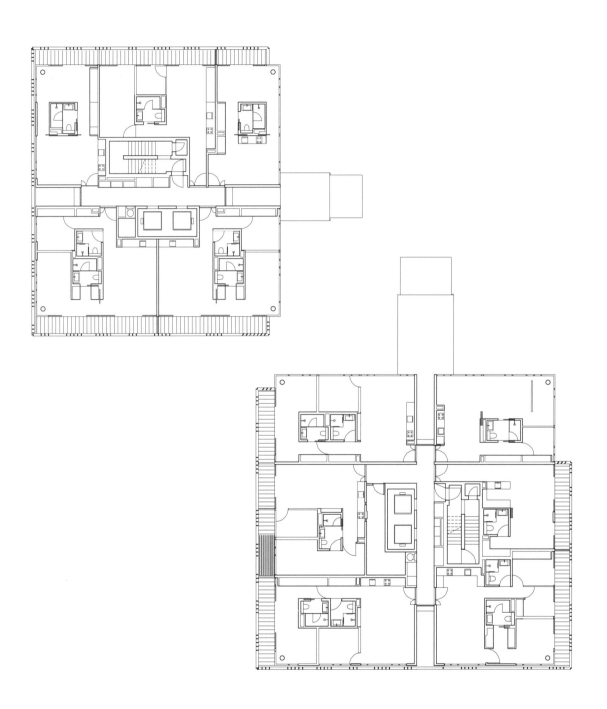

Petit Jervois

278    The surface fins lend interest and tempo to the simple building form.

# Spice Terraces

Revisiting the tropes of sustainability and storage

The façade's three-dimensional and monolithic expression leans more towards sculpture than building (above and opposite).

This house is the next iteration of Rene's – and by extension the firm's – personal thesis on dwelling. It rethinks the residential model's relationship with urban farming, the definition of enclosures and storage, and the possibilities and biographical role of the house in the display of the occupants' possessions. His former abode, House at Watten (pp. 24–29), presented a more abstract take on the modern tropical house, with a skewed air well and entirely white walls. In contrast, this house is ruled by a simple geometric framework, within which we rethought a house's possibilities, with sustainable living that incorporates urban farming and a double-skin enclosure, as well as storage design. Rene lives here with his wife and teenage daughter, whose needs from the old to the new home have also evolved.

We conceived the house holistically as a naturally breathing apparatus that reduces reliance on technology without compromising craftsmanship. The perfectly formed square box is cast in fair-faced concrete but disrupted by asymmetrical pushes and pulls in the façade. This results in a more open architecture than initially perceived. We employed a layered skin – glass behind concrete – to create an intermediary avenue for unbridled wind and sunlight. In between storeys, utilitarian steel grating aids passive upward ventilation. Water bodies edge the ground floor like a moat, cooling the adjacent common spaces and bestowing an atmosphere of tranquillity.

The placement, effects and removal of water are a topic for study in this house. Our belief in giving poetry to the mundane resulted in pronounced rainwater downspouts to channel water falling into pools like waterfalls on a rainy day, or into plants as both ecological and logical ways of landscape watering. We were influenced by the many inventive methods of removing water employed in Italian architect Carlo Scarpa's projects that celebrate rather than hide a building's workings.

Our design of this house bears similarities to the House at Watten in that the main spaces of both are dislocated from the party wall as an autonomous volume. The resultant cavity is excellent for heat transfer, passive airflow and natural light. In this home, it doubles as a linear garden for growing edible greens and spices, terraced to trace the topography of the interior

282    Edible gardening as an approach to decorative landscaping (above and above right).

staircase. This is one of several features that reflect an alternative approach to greening a house, including movable landscaping, in the form of a murraya hedge grown on the gate. These combined strategies reinforce our belief in biophilic principles of design inherent to living comfortably in a tropical environment.

This house's palette is simple and economical but the effects are no less rich than those of other projects specified with more expensive materials. Raw concrete walls, cement screeds on ceilings, reconstituted wood cladding, homogeneous tiles, as well as plywood and laminates for cabinetry juxtapose with Corten steel lookalike tiles, brightly coloured steel plates and coloured surfaces. It is a result of Rene's pursuit of ideas present in the legacies of Álvaro Siza and Le Corbusier – the former's quiet, rational forms and vernacular references, and the latter's recognizable use of colour and *béton brut* (raw concrete) – but with an added touch of irreverence and counterintuition.

For instance, we shaped the wet kitchen's ceiling into a vaulted form – a grand gesture typically reserved for cathedrals and museums – to emphasize its importance as the 'hub and engine' of the house. And yet this seriousness is undercut by a protruding laundry chute that takes the form of a tangerine-coloured cone. Idiosyncrasies such as these lead Rene to jest that another name for the project could have been 'House of Rejects' as it contains many unusual ideas rejected by his clients elsewhere.

Cabinetry plays a starring role in this house, replacing walls as a means to divide and define space. A plane of bookshelves parallels the climb of the staircase and spice terrace, connecting the different storeys in a less rigid way. In the detailing and construction of these components, we embraced the approach of a shipbuilder to insert storage functions into all kinds of leftover spaces. In the living room, we slotted a 'shoe sacristy' under the staircase; in the master bedroom on the first floor, we

explored new methods of wardrobe design with a circular 'bag baptistery' and double-volume 'clothing chapel'. These cabinets showcase the potential of plywood – at times as fair-faced plywood and other times topped with laminate. Such prudent materials have increasingly become part of our material library alongside marble, stone and timber. We also took a whimsical approach to cabinetry, for example a rotating shoe shelf at the entrance.

In its many iterations, we embraced storage as a form of biography, as it not only contains but also reflects the inhabitants' change in values and obsessions over the years. The house's joinery and 'carpentry-driven' interior design channels a holistic Bauhaus arts and crafts approach to designing a home. It also offers our office lessons not only in thinking outside the box but also in bringing delight to the intimate touchpoints of a habitat.

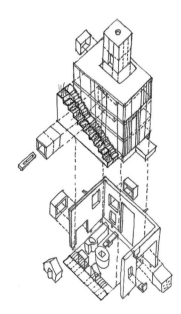

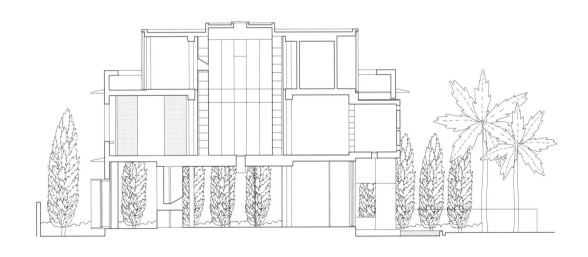

SECTION

0 1 2 5m

Ecological features include the architecture's double skin.

The house's proportions are predominantly classical in the sense that they deploy simple geometric ratios (above left and above right).

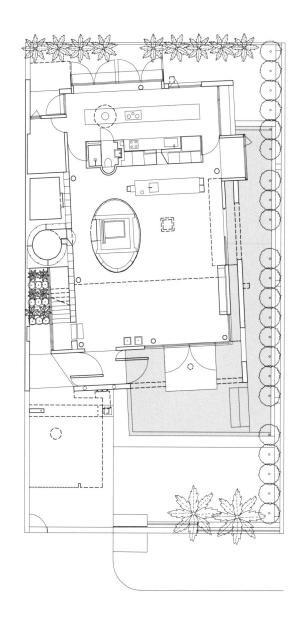

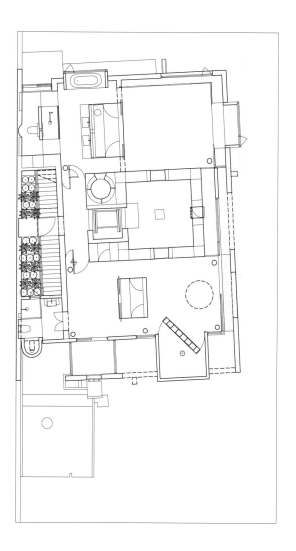

Rethinking the Tropical House    20 Years of RT+Q Architects

ATTIC PLAN

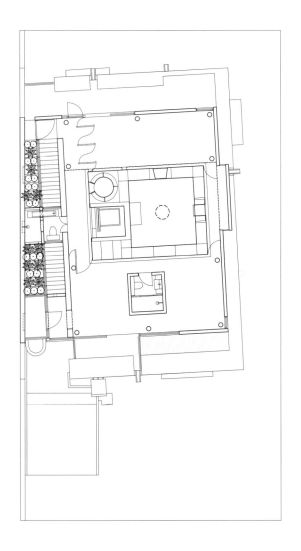

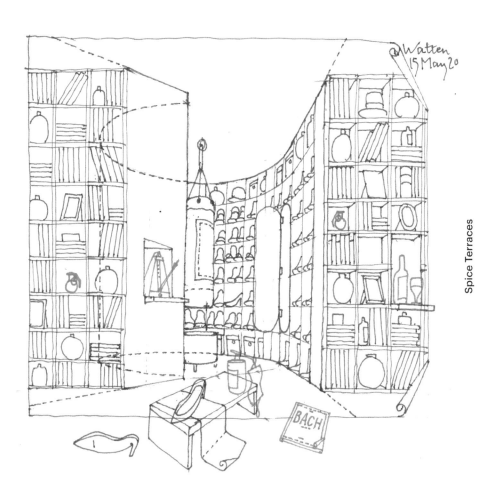

Spice Terraces

0  1  2       5m

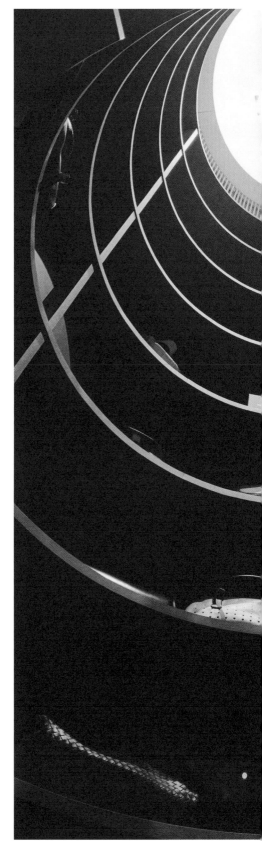

288    The 'shoe sacristy' (above), 'bag baptistery' (middle) and 'clothing chapel' (opposite).

Spice Terraces

View from a toilet in the attic to the staircase landing, framed by the three-storey bookshelf.

The house's double skin (above); the laundry chute in the kitchen (top); and the view from the attic into the 'clothing chapel' (bottom).

292    The material palette mixes rough and refined, warm and industrial.

A swivelling display in the daughter's room blurs the line between architecture and carpentry.

# House of Terracing Courtyards

A tectonic fissure opens up a ho

The staggered profile rethinks the conventional boxy courtyard outline.

An olive tree as sculpture in the courtyard (above); an architecture of precision (top); and a view of staggered balconies from the courtyard (bottom).

GROUND FLOOR PLAN

FIRST FLOOR PLAN

ATTIC PLAN

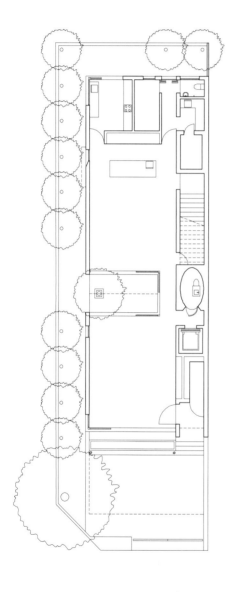

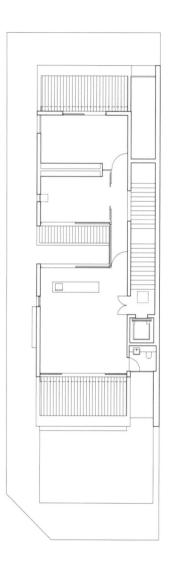

0  1  2          5m

Taking every opportunity to stretch the limits of studies in form, this house experiments with the corner terraced house typology that is defined by a large side wall. The main architectural scheme was a response to the long, rectilinear plot. We fractured this neatly composed plane and broke down its scale with a courtyard. The resulting staggered profile, like an abstracted crack, differs from the standard boxy courtyard outline. Two parallel surfaces in the courtyard cascade correspondingly to create this shape. One contains balconies on the upper levels and the other has overhangs that shadow a portion of the courtyard. These gestures together bring better illumination, ventilation and views into the house without the destructive forces of rain and water that are a common problem in the tropics.

The clients, who have three young children, wanted a home that embraced its proximity to the mature and verdant landscape of the neighbouring botanic gardens, whose thick green curtain of trees the house looks on to. Balconies extend the adjacent rooms to the outdoors, allowing residents to enjoy panoramic vistas of the surrounding greenery while maintaining a level of screening from the street. They also deflect the noise of the busy thoroughfare and roundabout outside rather than trapping it. Instead of opening up the house entirely – as is the natural inclination given the lush context – we designed an inward-looking dwelling by keeping the side elevation largely opaque to mitigate noise and offer privacy.

When the sliding, full-height glass doors around the courtyard are pushed aside, the living and dining rooms become one big open space. The void is framed by black steel C-channels (beams) and anchored by a small olive tree that gives the architecture a light touch. Services, storage spaces and the staircase are tucked along the party wall so that the main spaces are clean and functional. Within this spine, we carved out a guest bathroom whose oval plan is a delight to uncover within the house's boxy architecture.

This element of surprise is matched by another as one turns the wall to ascend the staircase. It is designed to be wider than typical residential staircases, so that the extra floor area encourages users to pause and linger with a book or, with children, to play and explore. It was inspired by Gian Lorenzo Bernini's Scala Regia – a flight of steps in Vatican City that forms part of the formal entrance to the Vatican in Rome. The house's staircase thus transmutes a peripheral and transitory area into a 'room' of its own. It is given added character with apertures in the wall between the staircase and corridors. Varied in size and use – as windows, balconies and lighting features – they enhance the connection between the two zones. A skylight cut neatly into the ceiling further brightens the space and bridges internal and external environments.

The external application of materials is considered from a point of mass versus skin, solid versus light. The boundary walls and side elevation are painted grey, emphasizing their opacity. In contrast, the front and rear elevations' aluminium-and-glass doors and façades give the residents control of light and views. The layout corresponds with the client's request for entertainment spaces but also private spaces for the children to go about their activities even when there are guests. The ground floor's common areas respond to that with the courtyard as a subtle divider. In the attic, this planning is echoed in the positioning of the family room upfront and the study area in the rear, both lightly connected through the courtyard. The clarity in plan is matched by the architecture's equally clear parti (key concept diagram), bringing together the variety of spatial demands into a coherent home.

SECTION

0  1  2      5m

298    The tectonics of the house correlates to the internal functions.

Shadow and light in the courtyard (top); the ovoid guest bathroom (bottom); and a staircase shaped by various apertures (above).

# Sentul Pavilion

A modern 'relic' in the landscape

This project rethinks the design of a garden pavilion.

Multi-Purpose Venue, Kuala Lumpur, Malaysia   2020–2022

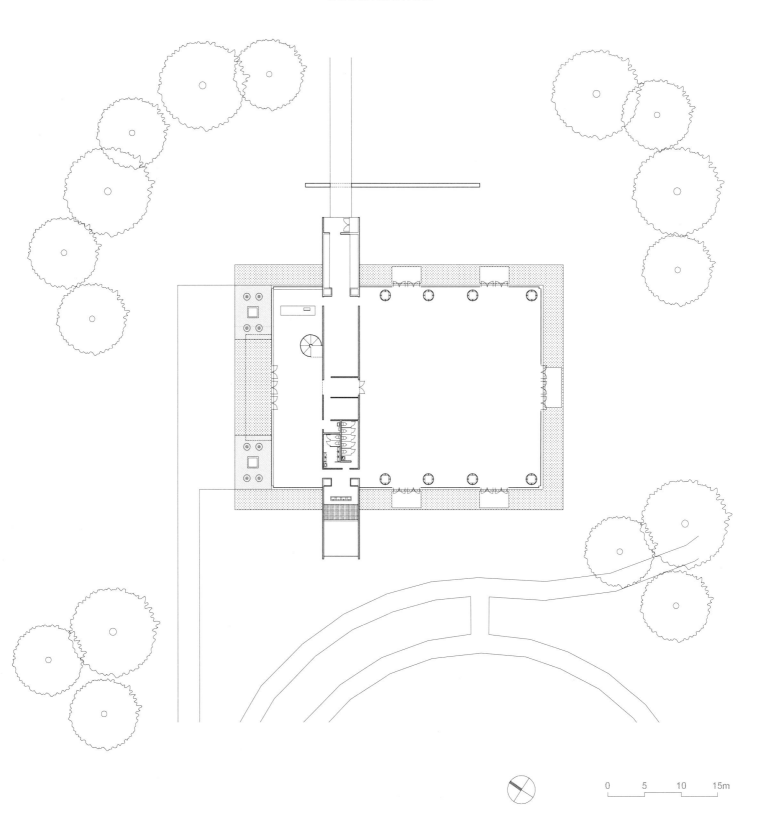

0   5   10   15m

Among the houses and condominiums in this monograph, this project sits like a sort of folly – ambiguous, malleable and set in bucolic environs. Our aim was to rethink the design of the garden pavilion, specifically one located prominently in a park that is part of the Sentul Masterplan by our client, a well-established Malaysian developer, for whom we had previously completed a series of projects. The 14-hectare (35-acre) green space is part of the rejuvenation of the neighbourhood that was once home to a thriving railway industry, until the Second World War left it destitute and abandoned. It is meant to serve the growing residential community springing up in the area and also as a green lung for all.

Within the park are several existing repurposed and newly built developments – including a performing arts centre, a library, a SoHo (small office/home office) and restaurants – that aim to promote business and trade to the newly gentrified area. The pavilion adds a garden setting to conferences that are usually held in urban settings, while serving as a community-building platform by offering facilities for cultural and social events such as weddings and concerts. Our design creates a sculptural object nestled in greenery. The aim was for a pavilion to exist as a 'shy' aberration of a building, almost dematerializing into its surroundings. Its form is simple, with no advertisements or embellishments, while its transparency and reflectivity celebrate the

nature that surrounds it. It is distinct in character but strives to have a strong connection to the land through its 'disappearance'. With the focus on the environment rather than on the edifice, it becomes a haven for the community to gather in.

The pavilion is located in a grassy clearing, enveloped by trees, with an existing pathway running around its perimeter. It is oriented to ensure the main space is set away from direct sunlight. The plan is 26.5 x 37 metres (87 x 121 feet) but the three-dimensional form is a triangulated building with a sloping roof that opens towards an existing tree line with views out to the expanse. Starting from a height of 5 metres (16 feet), it stretches upward to become an 18-metre-high (59-foot) atrium that captures the panorama of sky and greenery. With its visual transparency and volumetric impact, the atrium is intended to be, as Mies van der Rohe expresses, 'an ideal zone of tranquillity', and the distillation of a beautiful space.

A minimal construction of lithe steel framing and glass is deployed to protect visitors against the environment. Its rational and utilitarian design was inspired by Marc-Antoine Laugier's concept of 'the Primitive Hut', which has grounded many of our house designs (see pp. 102, 144 and 174). The pavilion contends that the ideal form embodies what is natural and intrinsic, where the architecture acts as a mediator between humans and nature. As an abstraction of Laugier's basic model, a simple sloping roof addresses the rain and the expansive glass

walls act as protection from the elements and insects, while allowing plenty of light and views. Its 'incomplete' wedge shape fosters a dialogue with the environment and provokes the imagination like a relic of the landscape. The proportion and scale of this composition were guided by our modernist approach to symmetry, while the exposed structure was painted white to express the purity and symmetry of the grid of the steel framing.

An elongated 45 x 5-metre (147½ x 16-foot) rectilinear block bisects the main block, demarcating two zones, one smaller than the other. This embodies a suggested procession from an intimate space into an expansive main hall, with the height of the pavilion following suit. The block, which protrudes out of the square, anchors the form and houses service spaces such as a kitchen, green rooms (lounges for performers and speakers) and storage spaces. At one end, a miniature environment is created in the bathroom, with an outdoor sink area nestled within an internal garden. A moon gate, an element we frequently employ to frame views and create interest in the architecture, opens the space and composes views of a sculptural bonsai tree within.

Overall, the free plan of the atrium allows for flexibility in the planning while serving as a destination that promotes usage of the park. This pavilion that celebrates life will also, it is hoped, facilitate the connection between humans and nature.

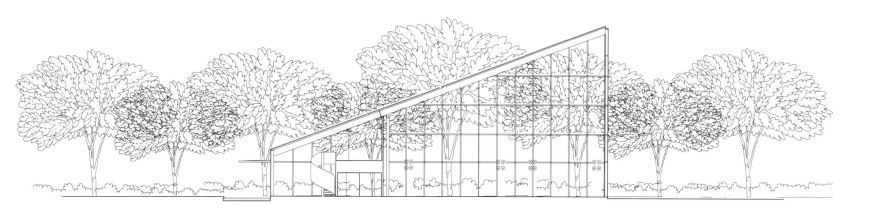

SECTION

0 2 5 10m

The sloping roof opens up towards an existing tree line with views out to the expanse.

The skeletal structure and reflective façade allow the pavilion to disappear into the landscape.

A spiral staircase painted in bronze provides a sensuous focal point in the pure space.

A piece of manicured nature is celebrated in the form of a bonsai tree in the bathroom.

The pavilion's orientation ensures that it does not receive direct sun in the main space.

The space within is intended, as Mies van der Rohe puts it, as 'an ideal zone of tranquillity'.

# Composing a Creative Practice

—Mok Wei Wei

Principal, W Architects, Singapore

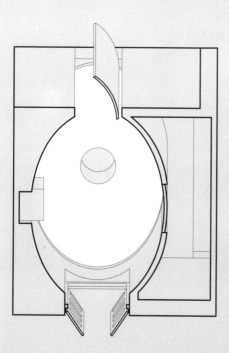

Rarely do you hear of an architect who does not have a designated desk in the office. Yet this is the basis that underlies Rene's unique working style at RT+Q Architects. Moving around the drawing studio with a pointer in hand, he comments and discusses with his architects, tracking the development of each design intensely. He himself designs by drawing beautiful sketches – be it a concept diagram, an axonometric massing or a tightly composed view of an interior space. In his own words, 'a self-respecting architect must do everything himself'. He also commits every Saturday morning to inspecting all the office's ongoing site projects, inviting staff to join him 'in the spirit of learning', as he likes to emphasize.

Many exquisite houses have been produced by this working method, developing a building typology that dominates RT+Q's portfolio from the last two decades. The designs of these houses have managed to avoid the trap of repetition and staleness. They adhere to a set of aesthetic values that are anchored by the respect for order, upon which the spirit of exploration makes its rhythmic dance.

Rene double-majored at Yale University – music and architecture. I'd like to think of these beautiful houses as musical compositions, created by an architect who has internalized the understanding of Western musical structures and makes a very tangible connection between music and his architecture. They are also a testament to the firm's commitment to the notion of architecture as a form of plastic, sculptural art, expressed in distinct forms, pure shapes and clear lines.

The creative spirit of RT cannot be fully realized without a base established by Q – Quek Tse Kwang, a founding partner of the firm. An avid collector of contemporary Southeast Asian art, Quek shares with Rene the same passion for good design, and manages the office in ways that reconcile economic viability with design quality.

Together, they keep the firm small and show us that the way a design-oriented practice stays relevant is not necessarily achieved by increasing the scale and diversity of its projects, but by keeping, at its core, a creative flame burning.

# Counter-Intuitive Design

—Kelley Cheng

Founder and Creative Director, The Press Room, Singapore

As a rite of passage, when a new architect or intern joins RT+Q Architects, they have to build a Le Corbusier model based on documented drawings from books. This custom has gone on for so many years that the practice had enough models to organize an exhibition. 'Le Corbusier 101' was a travelling show in 2022 featuring exactly 101 models of the architect's work – apparently the largest collection of Le Corbusier's models in the world.

It is an understatement to say that RT+Q's body of work shows its Corbusian lineage. Hence, to understand the practice's works, you must first understand Le Corbusier's works. To understand Le Corbusier's works, you must understand his five points of architecture. To understand his five points of architecture, you must understand modernist architecture.

Form follows function; new materials; open plans; clean lines; strong geometry; and a spirit of breaking away from conventions: these are typical of modernist architecture. The modern movement was born out of a desire to completely break away from classical architecture – as well as from neoclassical architecture, which was the wishy-washy in-between. The modern movement swooped in and basically said, 'To hell with it!' It was a real game-changer in the world of architecture from the 1920s to the 1950s, and architects today are still deeply influenced by its principles and philosophies. RT+Q is certainly one of the many that are flying the modern movement flag high, but with a dash of its own DNA – resulting in a new language that, for lack of a less clichéd term, might be called 'tropical modernism'.

And in the spirit of breaking away from conventions, Rene Tan has a funny theory that he instils in all his architects. To paraphrase him, it is that everyone has a habitual way of designing and you could allow that as the first step in the process, but once you see what you are inclined to design, the next step is to deliberately think of a less convenient proposition. This spirit of making his team not do what they are used to is what drives the practice's constant search for new design languages. If I could make a bumper sticker for RT+Q, it would say 'Counter-Intuitive Design', or maybe just 'CID'. It is a term that Rene himself actually coined half-jokingly during one of the lunches I had with him and his team of CIDs (Counter-Intuitive Designers).

Within this 'anti-kneejerk' design framework, the works of RT+Q have a few recurring motifs. That brings us to the five points of architecture by Le Corbusier: pilotis, roof gardens, open floor plans, long windows and open façades. These five elements are used frequently – perhaps not all at once – for each project by the practice alongside some of its signature motifs, including the spiral staircase, the gable roof, the overhanging roof, the double- or triple-volume space, and the bridge. Over and above these tangible elements, there is always that intangible touch of well-proportioned and elegantly composed façades. This is perhaps the Italian classicist inside Rene coming through. This sense of natural rhythm and '*stile italiano*' are reminders that he was originally trained as a classical pianist at Yale, only to find his real calling in architecture when he hurt his hand and started taking courses in the subject.

To say that the works of RT+Q are rooted in the rudiments of music is an understatement. In music, a motif is the smallest unit that contains thematic material. This means it is not an entire song or movement; nor is it a single note. But the motif is essential in conveying the overall identity of the piece. Most motifs are melodic, rhythmic and harmonic – the exact qualities that you can see and feel in the works of RT+Q.

Beyond the beautiful architecture that the practice will be remembered for, its legacy will be the friendship, warmth and generosity that it has shared with so many. From being a strong advocate in architectural education – the whole team is involved in running design studios in the Singapore University of Technology and Design and the National University of Singapore – to the many dinners it hosts for industry peers, students and friends. The practice also has a close-knit relationship among its members and a respectful succession plan from founders TK Quek to Rene, and to the next generation led by TK's son, Jon. Such professional kinship is priceless and inimitable. It can only be admired and not understood for many. However, what we can try to learn and understand is perhaps its architecture.

Before you study this book, you will have to understand the modern movement, Le Corbusier, classical architecture, and yes, even Chopin and Beethoven.

And these would be essential in the appreciation of RT+Q 101.

# Architecture and More

*Luo Jingmei in conversation with Rene Tan, Quek Tse Kwang (TK), Jonathan Quek, Koh Sock Mui, Koh Kai Li and Tiw Pek Hong of RT+Q Architects*

### On Direction

**Rene and TK, do you recall the first time you were amazed by a piece of architecture?**

Rene:   Although born in Terengganu, I grew up in Penang, Malaysia. Like Singapore, it was a former British colonial port. I marvelled at the neo-brutalist buildings of the 1950s and 1960s in Penang, particularly the Island Girls' School, Bangunan Tuanku Syed Putra (a government office building) and the Dewan Sri Pinang multi-purpose hall. I also admired the Dewan Bahasa dan Pustaka (Institute of Language and Literature), the Dewan Tunku Canselor (Tunku Chancellor Hall) at the University of Malaysia, and Ken Yeang's 'Roof-Roof House' in Kuala Lumpur. I was impressed by the unapologetic rigour of the designs, which combined early ideas of sustainability and openness in planning. These buildings honoured the legacies of modernism.

I was also fascinated by models of buildings, and intrigued by the act of constructing them. I grew up obsessed with Airfix models, scale replicas of aircraft, battleships and so on. This childhood obsession has never left me. In fact, I have just bought the model of the Second World War battleship Bismarck. In retrospect, I got into architecture comparatively late. I went to college intending to pursue music and to become a concert pianist, so I always describe myself as an 'accidental architect'.

TK:   As a student, I was lucky to go on an exchange programme in the USA, where I visited Frank Lloyd Wright's celebrated house Fallingwater in Pennsylvania. To me, it is still Wright's crowning architectural statement in organic architecture, in how it integrates human needs, architecture and nature.

**Like many Singapore architecture practices of your generation, RT+Q Architects initially used houses as vehicles of expression, producing varied interpretations of the 'tropical modern house'. While others have since moved on to larger projects, RT+Q Architects has steadfastly worked mainly on houses over the last twenty years. Why so?**

Rene:   More than any other building typology, the house continues to present a great, continual and enlarged challenge. The needs of families today are expanding so rapidly. Just when we think we've designed our most interesting house, the brief for the next project surprises us. The briefs have also become more ambitious. But we don't wave away these challenges; we embrace them.

Airbitat Oasis Smart Bus Stop prototype

Stage set for *The Telephone* and *La Voix Humaine*

Regardless, we hope to continue to create meaningful architecture, even if it's just houses.

Houses are a personal idiosyncrasy too. The composer Frédéric Chopin never wrote symphonies or operas, but he is among the greatest musicians of the Western tradition. He wrote twenty-seven études, of which twenty-four (comprising two separate collections, Op. 10 and Op. 25) are the more known, and twenty-four preludes (Op. 28) – good works that exhaust the full spectrum of problems and issues despite their small size. As the great Ukraine-born pianist Vladimir Horowitz said, there can be more music in a short mazurka than in a long symphony.[1] Likewise, there can be more literature in an eight-line poem than an eight-volume epic novel. So we won't mind if RT+Q's legacy is as a firm known for smaller works, like a poet. I guess this brings us back to the idea that we may never get out of doing houses.

TK: Well, people have seen our houses and like them, so we continue to design them. Houses are the heart and soul of their owners. Don't forget, there are the limitations of their land and budget, so it's very personal. And we have very nice clients who thank us for our hard work, sending us text messages to say they're happy with their house. It's nice to hear that our hard work pays off.

Rene: Actually, we have done some larger jobs. For example, we completed the Petit Jervois condominium in Singapore (pp. 268–279), some developments in Kuala Lumpur, such as Shorefront (pp. 78–87) and Sentul East (pp. 88–99), and a few in Indonesia as well. We are also now designing a condominium in China. And I dare say, if moving on indeed means doing other things beyond houses, we have also done a lot of other things, even tombstones and stage sets.

**Let's talk about some of these smaller works. How do they embody the essence of the firm's ethos and methods?**

Pek Hong: Smaller projects are interesting as they let us apply the same principles and vigour that we put into the designs of houses on a different scale. While the process is similar, the outcome differs, as the needs are different. However, no matter how small the details are – be it a door handle of the guest bathroom in one of our houses, or the bench seat divider of the Airbitat Oasis Smart Bus Stop prototype – it has been ingrained in us that these designs should be not only functional, but also aesthetically pleasing, and perhaps even embody a sense of playfulness.

Jonathan: Smaller projects keep the design work in our office fresh. They take us out of our comfort zone as we apply our knowledge of design to varying typologies while expanding our range of work. I think there is an unspoken effort to aspire, to design everything and anything without being too self-conscious, and to be consummate in our approach to design.

Rene: The short answer is: we design for everyone in every circumstance. People always ask us, how many GCBs (Good Class Bungalows)[2] have you designed? But we don't just design GCBs.

TK: In fact, we are design driven, not commercially driven.

Rene: You ask us to design anything – a stage set, a tombstone – and we'll do it. The tombstone embodies the clarity of form – not the purity of the cube, but the clarity and discernibility of the cubic model.

=DREAMS Campus at Haig Road

A 'Home' in Choa Chu Kang

The stage sets embody our reverence for Baroque architecture. In both stage sets we recently designed, we employed the concept of false perspective, which is a well-known device used for theatrical settings. Some precedents are the corridor in Palazzo Spada designed by Francesco Borromini, and Andrea Palladio's Teatro Olimpico (Olympic Theatre), which made the actors look larger than life. As in our houses, we make use of our knowledge of history in the designs.

Another project important to us is =DREAMS in Haig Road, Singapore. The project adapted and repurposed the former Geylang Serai Community Club into a first-of-its-kind weekday residence with educational facilities for children from low-income households.

Kai Li:    At the =DREAMS campus project, it was interesting and meaningful for us to apply our knowledge and experience from working on private residential homes to a community project with a different set of users and stakeholders. While the selection of materials and finishes for the project differed from what we were commonly used to, scale, proportion and hierarchy remained the core design values.

### On Influences

**In 2022, RT+Q embarked on another kind of project – an exhibition of your collection of Le Corbusier building models made by interns that have passed through your office. From the forty-five models shown at the first exhibition, there were more than 150 pieces showcased at recent exhibitions. Why is this exhibition so important for the firm?**

Rene:    It's the logical conclusion to our years of acquiring and disseminating our knowledge of Le Corbusier in particular and architecture in general – definitely the most encyclopaedic of modern architects. This exhibition is close to my heart because a lot of my learning about Le Corbusier took place while teaching at Syracuse University, where I first met TK. What do we do with this knowledge? It is meaningful to share it with the world! It's very exciting for us. It's our form of 'educational philanthropy'.

**Why do you get your interns to make the models?**

Rene:    Every intern who comes into the practice – be it for one month or two years – spends the first week making a model of a Le Corbusier building. This is the best way to introduce them to a piece of world-class architecture, instead of making them dabble with odd jobs in the office. Even though the interns use a 3D printer, they have to construct the digital model first and then assemble the pieces by hand. They have to measure, draw and think about every corner of the work. It is a way of guiding the interns. They also cultivate a sense of belonging by being part of this larger vision.

The value of the collection is not even about the known works of Le Corbusier, like Villa Savoye, but his unbuilt, unfinished and unknown ones. Can you imagine suddenly showcasing to the world the unpublished works of Shakespeare, and people realizing he was not just writing tragic plays and romantic comedies but also other things? When you ask people about Le Corbusier, they can list Villa Savoye, Villa Stein, Ronchamp, but he also designed many less celebrated buildings, such as La Cité de Refuge for the Salvation Army and Les Constructions 'Murondins' – a scheme to erect provisional housing and villages that he later unsuccessfully campaigned to be built for war refugees.

*Architecture: A Day in the Life of Le Corbusier* (2021) Archifest/Alliance Française de Singapour exhibition

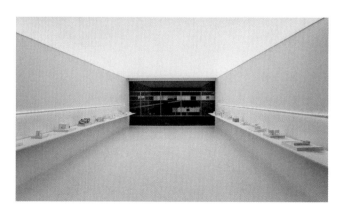

*Le Corbusier Unbuilt Projects* (2022) exhibition at Kopimanyar in Indonesia

**The firm's work is grounded on a strong foundation of classical and modern architecture. What are some of the ways the firm applies lessons from the past?**

Rene: By making reference to the past in terms of geography so that one can locate our works in the continuum of history and place. Memory of tradition and place is important. For instance, the oculus in some of the bathrooms in our houses recalls the Pantheon in Rome, and the circular apertures of Chinese gardens. That's also why we teach, separately from our regular work at the office. In one course, we studied the works of Adolf Loos and Otto Wagner in Vienna; in another, we studied the works of Gian Lorenzo Bernini and Borromini in Rome.

**How does the notion of order co-exist with the firm's approach of counterintuition, of rethinking architectural convention? Can you answer this with reference to the works of Le Corbusier and Palladio, whom you often look to?**

Rene: Order is an elusive idea – elusive because it is only meaningful if 'tempered', i.e. it cannot exist alone; it needs, in musical terms,

rubato[3] for its conclusion. Palladio and Le Corbusier are important references for us as one is a result of the other. Scholars have pointed out how, for instance, Villa La Rotonda by Palladio and Villa Savoye by Le Corbusier bear tripartite compositional similarities. They teach us about scale in the way architecture relates to the human body.

When we talk about counterintuition in tropical architecture, the intuition is to immediately focus on sustainable materials, cross-ventilation, screens, and so on. But who would think that Baroque architecture would be a source for our work? And why is it important? Because I think Baroque architecture gave us its legacy of nice forms, and we are interested in creating beautiful spaces. An example is the church of San Carlo alle Quattro Fontane (also called San Carlino) in Rome by Borromini. Why is this building important? Because I think it manipulates, liberates and manages space, both internally or externally. Nearby, the church of Sant'Andrea al Quirinale designed by Bernini also has beautiful spaces with great proportions, scale and light, which are alive with

movement and tension, employing the Baroque oval. My feeling is that all this architecture of 'clean lines' – modernism and all – is a thing of the past. I think modernism, when not well interpreted, can rob architecture of its richness.

**If that is the case, why do you still reference Le Corbusier's legacy?**

Rene: Oh, Le Corbusier is not just about modernism in the sense of straight lines; his works are also very sculptural and playful. They affect the human soul.

**You have also credited Robert Venturi's book *Complexity and Contradiction in Architecture* as a strong influence. Can you elaborate?**

Rene: Venturi was right to point out that through history, architecture has shown itself to be elusive of manifestos, rules and dogma. The richest examples of architecture are often 'messy' and transcend order – from the gardens of China to the temples of Egypt. As I have often believed, architecture can begin rationally in the mind, but must subsequently end in the heart. Architecture is a 'messy vitality', a

Rene speaking as part of the *Le Corbusier Maquettes: The Representation of Modern Architecture* (2022) exhibition in Penang, Malaysia

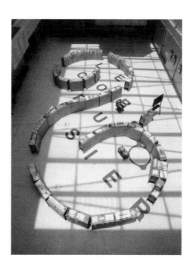

*Le Corbusier 101: An Exhibition Over Space and Time* (2022) exhibition at the National Design Centre, Singapore

personification of life itself and of the vagaries of the human condition. Postmodernism is memory-driven, and tropical architecture is weather-driven. Our work hopes to combine both.

**How do some of the firm's projects employ that contrarian streak that Venturi promulgates, in rethinking the normalized way of programming domestic architecture or experiencing space?**

Rene: In one word, counterintuition. The best examples: putting bridges instead of paintings in a space designed for artwork in House with a Sanctum (pp. 204–217); and putting a vaulted ceiling – traditionally reserved for monumental architecture – in the wet kitchen, such as in Spice Terraces (pp. 280–293). Both projects elude dogma, and eschew rules and regulation.

**It's interesting how the firm's references to architecture have broadened and become less dogmatic over the past twenty years.**

Rene: Ideas change but intuitions don't. The intuition to create beautiful spaces, which I believe must remain the primary concern of architecture, has remained because beautiful spaces can elevate the human spirit. This is a prerequisite of all good architecture. The ideas of how to achieve this have continually evolved as we are constantly learning and rethinking. I think our work has evolved. We started out being more 'modern' because we were schooled that way, but we are now more 'baroque' as we have unschooled ourselves to be more receptive to other methods along the journey. We have also put aside dogmas and tried not to think like architects. In short, we have become more open.

## Dissecting the RT+Q House

**The projects in this book are organized roughly chronologically to show the development of the firm's designs. But you have also described in *Contemporaneous Architecture Singapore* that 'RT+Q's oeuvre comprises three approaches: the abstract form, the Primitive Hut and contemporary tropical houses. While these approaches are different in form, they share a common DNA, which we call "core values".' What are these 'core values'?**

Rene: They are proportion and scale – inherent values in any epoch. They are values of an architecture of humanism. I think our work is very broad. We design everything. We've got pitched-roof houses, abstract cubes, an ovoid house, and more. I think it's important, as TK once said humorously, that we can do filet mignon as well as *char kway teow*.[4]

**Was the design of one of the firm's first projects, House at Holland (pp. 14–23), a reaction against the prevailing Balinese forms of the 1990s in Singapore that attempted to recreate popular resort architecture?**

Rene: I don't think it was a reaction, but I certainly thought that the abstract approach could be an alternative solution to tropical architecture. When I first came to Singapore in the mid-1990s, the Balinese style appeared to be the prevailing trend. I was trained in the more abstract approach, referencing architects like Louis Kahn all the time. We didn't have a large body of work done in this

House of the Twins

House at Watten

abstract tropical way to draw upon so that forced us to think harder.

**Was it the Svarga Residence (pp. 102–113) in Bali that initiated the firm's exploration into the monolithic, pitched-roof form as a contemporary demonstration of the Primitive Hut?**

Rene: Yes, it started with that project. The notion of the Primitive Hut is not as old as the phrase connotes. What it really means is a simple dwelling of essentials – namely, columns, roof and enclosure – that any epoch needs. The firm is very conscious of this because the work that we hope to produce is of 'bare essentials' and free from decorative excesses.

**What distinguishes the firm's abstract houses from those in the contemporary tropical category?**

Rene: Under 'Abstraction', our architecture is more geometric in nature. These houses eschew references to the classical idiom. Some examples are Spice Terraces and House with a Sanctum. Our contemporary tropical houses are more weather-driven. The architecture clearly has rain- and heat-defying elements, and devices like deep overhanging eaves, sun-shading canopies and heat-mitigating screens. Some examples are House at Pondok Indah (pp. 60–69), the Art Collector's House (pp. 132–143) and the Petit Jervois apartments.

**The firm's works have developed organically in response to the clients' briefs, contexts and the trajectory of your personal architectural preoccupations. Is the recent emphasis on Baroque influences taking shape as a fourth category in the firm's oeuvre?**

Rene: Yes. Baroque forms with figural spaces, often with curves and oval shapes, are showing up more in our work. As I mentioned, modern architecture can rob architecture of its potential richness. Employing these Baroque gestures will restore spatial and formal drama to architecture.

**I would like you to explain some elements in the firm's architecture that I have observed. Some bursts of colour have started to appear in later works, such as House with a Sanctum, House with Twin Gardens (pp. 238–247) and Spice Terraces. Can you expound on this straying away from neutral and natural palettes to these hued experiments? What does it do for the house – spatially, emotionally, and so on?**

Rene: The 'straying' part came primarily through two sources. One, I have always been fascinated with colour as it presents opportunities to highlight and emphasize certain elements of architecture. And two, I think it's also a response to trying to create architecture that doesn't look only at natural materials like stone or timber for colour; painting using colour is sometimes a more economical option. Colour can also affect the emotions. For instance, in House with a Sanctum, we used turquoise paint to illuminate a stair coming up from the basement to create a calming effect while one ascends it.

**Another device the firm has started to experiment with is interior windows that look from one internal space into another. In Spice Terraces, one can look from the walk-in wardrobe on the first floor into the living room on the ground floor through an aperture. Why are they employed?**

Double 'C' House

A painting by Rene

Rene: They are elements of surprise that enliven the built environment. We think architecture can be about discoveries, surprises and rediscoveries in memory. We hope to create architecture that can reinvent itself while staying relevant and engaging for different users and across different times.

We see this as a form of sustainability. We believe the conditions of 'sustainability' ought not be limited to heat management, green solutions, energy consumption and recyclable materials – provisions that buildings in the tropics would have already met. In many ways, sustainability of memory, of the mind and of emotions is also important in our work. The ability of spaces to liberate, to reflect and to rediscover themselves is important. We see this as a form of experiential sustainability. We call this 'phenomenal sustainability' – as opposed to 'literal sustainability'.

**Can you expound on how you create a sense of order in the planning of spaces?**

Rene: We try to 'define' spaces without 'defying' spatiality, without denying space the ability to liberate itself. This way of designing gives users a sense of enclosure but still allows room for one to manoeuvre and free oneself from the space. It is achieved through using walls to suggest a formal perimeter but not totally enclosing it. House at Holland, Petit Jervois, Spice Terraces and House with Twin Gardens all exhibit this.

**A gesture I've noticed even in earlier works is the technique of cutting narrow apertures into walls at their edges or corners.**

Rene: It has become a design strategy in keeping with our approach of 'putting the right thing in the wrong place'. It helps us with creating surprises in the work we do. An aperture helps to break the scale down, especially in larger surfaces and buildings. This is also an attempt to restore composition to the making of architecture. I believe that many of us have forgotten about this. I have always told people that I like our buildings to look 'incomplete'. Now that I am painting more and more, I realize these ideas are also resurfacing in my paintings. The incompleteness in creating compositions is important whether in art or architecture because it will suggest the next idea for you. That came from Michael Graves. So don't make things look too perfect. Even if it has to suffer a little 'accident', let it be.

### On Mentorship and Education

**Academia is clearly a pillar of the firm, both in the grounding for the firm's projects as well as in Rene's role as an educator at the Singapore University of Technology and Design (SUTD) and the National University of Singapore (NUS) that involves the senior colleagues. Why is this important?**

Jonathan: Teaching gives us an outlet to go back and explore those subjects we learned in school all those years ago. Through it, we dig through the academic books and inspiring articles. We re-educate ourselves with timeless plans that we apply to our work. For example, the carving out of pochés[5] for baptismal fonts in Baroque churches has inspired unique wardrobe spaces or unexpected cove details in the 'wasted spaces' of our bathroom designs.

Study trip to Venice, Italy, 2014

Study trip to Le Corbusier's grave, France, 2015

Study trip to Indian Institute of Management Ahmedabad, India, 2016

**Rene and TK clearly have a good rapport with the staff. What are their mentoring styles?**

Kai Li: Rene selflessly shares his knowledge and site experience through our regular site visits. He often reminds us that if we observe carefully, the answers can be found in our surroundings. His flexibility and adaptability towards problem solving has enabled me to approach challenges as opportunities so as to create unique and engaging architecture.

On the other hand, TK inspires and encourages us with anecdotes about his past experience as a young architect. His clarity of thought and attention to detail have also helped us sharpen the way we communicate with our project teams. They both take a personal interest in each one of us, allowing us to grow personally and professionally.

Pek Hong: Yes, Rene constantly imparts his knowledge of the arts, history and music to us. It is common in the office for him to spontaneously call for everyone's attention to highlight a new book he bought or a new idea of his. On the other hand, TK is quick to guide us in the ins and outs of managing clients, contracts and projects. For newcomers, TK always gets them into his office to brief them on the nuances of project management. These are sadly not taught to us in school and can only be learned through the experiences of our seniors and ourselves.

Sock Mui: My first project was a bungalow for a family of four. Coming from a background in commercial architecture, I was blown away by how detailed the designs were from the first meeting. Very quickly, I realized that that is how Rene works. He studies massing and comes up with contextual responses quickly and effectively through thumbnail axonometric sketches and detailed plans. Every design study offers a different option for a beautiful space, or spaces. Working through designs with Rene is a lesson in proportions that one can never learn based on theory. Regardless of style and type of architecture, proportion is the constant that all good architecture needs.

Jonathan: TK and Rene inspired me to find meaning through design, and taught me that one can leave an indelible legacy on society through this profession – something not many others can claim.

**Rene and TK, you have kept your office relatively small through the past twenty years. Today, the staff count is still a modest twenty. Do you have plans to expand the team?**

Rene: We have worked hard to keep the office to a size that we think we can manage properly. TK has mentioned before that one partner or principal can only effectively manage a ratio of one to ten to maintain the quality of the work. This is very important and is what keeps us focused, and smallish as an office.

TK: I often wonder about the difficulties of running a big office. Compared to big firms, where their leaders might not know what all 200 staff are working on, we are very involved. My door is always open. If you come in, you either get praise, a scolding or a raise. [Laughs] But I enjoy my work very very much.

**How else do you inspire your staff?**

Rene: In many ways. First is getting them to share in the accolades that the firm receives. Number two is getting them involved in the work. I think a

RT+Q office

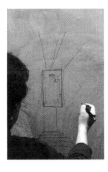

Drawing on-site

Site visit to Widya Chandra

house is a manageable project from start to finish to give them a sense of ownership.

TK: Each of our colleagues is given a house to design. We had a Korean colleague who remembers us fondly because of this. He previously worked for a big firm in New York, but it was only when he joined us that he finally completed his first project – a house. He told his parents, who came to see it. They were so happy that he did it practically on his own. That's the kind of useful experience people who work with us benefit from.

Sock Mui: I agree. I find meaning and delight in seeing a project through from lines on paper to the physical building, in seeing details that we have laboured over, proportions that we may have worked over and over – or even argued and fought for – come to life and be enjoyed by the people for whom they were designed. A client shared that her grandchildren are now very keen to visit her new house as the architecture allows for fun. As Rene says, 'putting the right thing in the wrong place' allows users to engage with our architecture.

Rene: I hope it comes across that we are rather generous with – TK,

what's the word? – disseminating knowledge and sharing with our colleagues the concept of fun and good work in architecture. Many of them came to my home to watch the World Cup final together. It is part of our mentoring approach. I hope everyone realizes how much football is like architecture in the way it too manages space.

TK: Like I always say, if I can make a particularly good plate of *char kway teow*, I will try to teach them instead of letting the secret die with me because I hope they can make a better *char kway teow* next time. There's no purpose in keeping secrets. Their generation should be better than us, and the next better than them.

Rene: In another example, our colleagues will become ambassadors for RT+Q Architects and our travelling Le Corbusier exhibition, where we will sometimes get them to give a talk. This gives them an opportunity to travel and to be identified with something that is global. It will help give them a sense of belonging and empowerment. The efforts of our colleagues are important. So this monograph should not be all about Rene Tan and Quek Tse Kwang, but also about all these other people who had a big role. It's teamwork.

Endnotes

1  As quoted by Vladimir Horowitz: 'Sometimes,' he says, 'there can be more music in [a] five-minute piece than in [a one-hour] piece. A mazurka of Chopin can be greater than [a] symphony of Mahler.' Helen Epstein, 'The Grand Centric of the Concert Hall', *The New York Times* (8 January 1978), https://www.nytimes.com/1978/01/08/archives/the-grand-eccentric-of-the-concert-hall-horowitz.html

2  Good Class Bungalows sit in the most prestigious segment of Singapore's property market thanks to their limited number, high cost and larger size. They are typically defined as having a minimum plot size of 1,400 square metres (15,000 square feet) and being not more than two storeys high (excluding basements and attics). They are located in one of thirty-nine residential areas in Singapore designated by the state as Good Glass Bungalow Areas, which have strict constraints to preserve the exclusivity and low-rise character of the neighbourhood.

3  A technique in music by which a performer deviates from the rhythms written by the composer, altering them to give more expression to a performance.

4  A beloved local noodle dish.

5  An architectural term used to define the inhabitable spaces inside walls and columns, which typically contain mechanical or plumbing services. In drawings, they are blackened with solid or dark colours to indicate which part of the building they have been cut into. Many Baroque buildings manipulate poché to become a key spatial element, with the pochéd spaces as important as the rooms themselves. In the works of RT+Q Architects, they have been appropriated into usable spaces such as niches and walk-in shoe cabinets.

A 2016 Christmas party

Models are an important medium in the office's pursuit of proportion, scale and clarity of form.

# Chronology

2003–2005
House at Frankel
Singapore
*Detached House*

2003–2004
House at Jalan Tarum
Singapore
*Detached House*

2003–2005
House at Kovan
Singapore
*Detached House*

2003–2005
House at Kembangan
Singapore
*Semi-Detached House*

2003–2007
House at Buckley
Singapore
*Detached House*

2003–2005
House at Queen Astrid Park
Singapore
*Good Class Bungalow[1]*

2003–2009
House at Damansara
Kuala Lumpur, Malaysia
*Detached House*

See pages 42 to 49

2004–2006
House at Holland
Singapore
*Detached House*

See pages 14 to 23

2004–2007
House off Bukit Timah
Singapore
*Detached House*

2005
Everton Road
Singapore
*Residential Interior*

2005
Xavier Apartment
Singapore
*Residential Interior*

2005–2007
Houses at Sundridge Park I & II
Singapore
*Detached Houses*

2005
Wine Garage
Singapore
*Commercial Interior*

2005–2009
Paterson Linc
Singapore
*Condominium*

2005–2008
Houses at Camden I, II & III
Singapore
*Good Class Bungalows*

2005–2007
House at Dunearn
Singapore
*Detached House*

2005–2008
House off Farrer
Singapore
*Detached House*

2005–2007
House at Trevose
Singapore
*Detached House*

2005–2010
House at Ford
Singapore
*Detached House*

2005–2007
House at Namly
Singapore
*Semi-Detached House*

2006–2010
d7
Kuala Lumpur, Malaysia
*Mixed-Use Development*

See pages 88 to 99

2006–2018
Shorefront
Penang, Malaysia
*Condominium*

See pages 78 to 87

2006–2007
House at Sunset
Singapore
*Detached House*

2006–2008
Double 'C' House
Singapore
*Detached House*

See pages 30 to 41

2006–2010
House at Chestnut
Singapore
*Detached House*

2006–2008
House at Kebayoran Bahru
Jakarta, Indonesia
*Detached House*

2006–2009
Houses at Jalan Bahasa
Singapore
*Cluster Housing*

2006–2007
House at Thomson
Singapore
*Semi-Detached House*

2006–2011
d6
Kuala Lumpur, Malaysia
*Mixed-Use Development*

See pages 88 to 99

2006–2011
d7 Bridge
Kuala Lumpur, Malaysia
*Bridge*

See pages 88 to 99

2006–2014
The Capers
Kuala Lumpur, Malaysia
*Condominium*

See pages 88 to 99

2006–2008
House at Fernhill
Singapore
*Detached House*

2007–2009
House at Cable
Singapore
*Conserved Detached House*

See pages 50 to 59

2007–2009
House at Vanda I & II
Singapore
*Detached Houses*

2007–2009
House at Pondok Indah
Jakarta, Indonesia
*Detached House*

See pages 60 to 69

2007–2008
House at Watten
Singapore
*Terraced House*

See pages 24 to 29

2007–2010
House at Cairnhill
Singapore
*Conserved Terraced House*

2007–2010
House at Pondok Indah II
Jakarta, Indonesia
*Detached House*

2008–2009
HSBC Lift lobby
Singapore
*Commercial Interior*

2008–2015
House at Pekan Nenas
Johor Bahru, Malaysia
*Detached House*

2008–2011
House at Gladiola
Singapore
*Detached House*

2008–2013
Green Collection
Singapore
*Cluster Housing*

2008–2012
House at Sentosa Cove
Singapore
*Detached House*

2008–2010
House at Vanda III
Singapore
*Detached House*

2009–2010
House at Pierce Road
Singapore
*Good Class Bungalow*
Addition & Alteration

2009–2011
House in Three Movements
Singapore
*Detached House*

See pages 70 to 77

2009–2011
House at Namly II
Singapore
*Semi-Detached House*

2009–2011
House at Oriole
Singapore
*Good Class Bungalow*

2009–2012
House at Holland II
Singapore
*Detached House*

2009–2011
House at Oriole II
Singapore
*Good Class Bungalow*

2009–2011
House at Sunset II
Singapore
*Detached House*

2009–2012
House at Seletar Hills
Singapore
*Semi-Detached House*

2010–2016
The Fennel
Kuala Lumpur, Malaysia
*Condominium*

2010–2011
House at Nim
Singapore
*Semi-Detached House*

2010–2012
House at Vanda IV
Singapore
*Semi-Detached House*

2010–2013
House at King Albert Park
Singapore
*Good Class Bungalow*

2010–2012
House at Seaview
Singapore
*Semi-Detached House*

2010–2014
House at Nassim
Singapore
*Good Class Bungalow*

2010–2013
House at Tai Hwan
Singapore
*Terraced House*

2010–2013
House at Sixth Avenue
Singapore
*Good Class Bungalow*

2010–2013
House on a Prairie
Singapore
*Detached House*

See pages 114 to 123

2010–2014
Mr Punch
Singapore
*Commercial Interior*

2011–2015
Senopati Suites 2
Jakarta, Indonesia
*Condominium*

2011–2012
Svarga Residence
Bali, Indonesia
*Detached House*

See pages 102 to 113

2011–2012
House at Siglap
Singapore
*Semi-Detached House*

2011–2018
House at Semarang
Semarang, Indonesia
*Detached House*

2011–2013
House at Kheam Hock
Singapore
*Detached House*

2011–2013
House at Oriole III
Singapore
*Good Class Bungalow*

2011–2014
House with Courtyards
Singapore
*Good Class Bungalow*
Reconstruction

2011–2015
Art Collector's House
Singapore
*Detached House*

See pages 132 to 143

2011–2012
House at Sunset III
Singapore
*Detached House*

2011–2013
Penthouse off Orchard
Singapore
*Residential Interior*

2011–2014
Houses with Cuts
Singapore
*Cluster Housing*

2011–2015
House of Generations
Singapore
*Good Class Bungalow*

2011–2015
House with Bridges
Singapore
*Detached House*

See pages 144 to 153

2011–2016
House at Pakubuwono
Jakarta, Indonesia
*Residential and Commercial*

2011–2014
House of the Connoisseur
Singapore
*Conserved Terrace House*

See pages 124 to 131

2011–2014
House at Cairnhill II
*Singapore*
*Conserved Terraced House*

2011–2015
Senopati Suites 3
Jakarta, Indonesia
*Condominium*

2011–2015
1945
Jakarta, Indonesia
*Commercial Interior*

2012–2015
Asiana Headquarters
Jakarta, Indonesia
*Commercial*

2012–2015
House at Tropicana
Selangor, Malaysia
*Detached House*

2012–2014
House at King's Close
Singapore
*Semi-Detached House*

2012–2014
House with a Twist
Singapore
*Terraced House*

2012–2018
Uthant Place
Kuala Lumpur, Malaysia
*Condominium*

2012–2014
House with an Impluvium
Singapore
*Detached House*

2012–2016
House at Matlock
Singapore
*Detached House*

2012–2014
House at Ming Teck Park
Singapore
*Semi-Detached House*

2012–2022
House at Widya Chandra
Jakarta, Indonesia
*Detached House*

2012–2016
House with Fins
Singapore
*Good Class Bungalow*

2012–2016
House with Shadows
Singapore
*Detached House*

See pages 174 to 187

2012–2016
House in Grey
Singapore
*Good Class Bungalow*

2012–2013
Emerald Bay – Puteri Harbour
Development Phase 3 & 4
Show Houses
Johor Bahru, Malaysia
*Detached Houses*

2013–2015
House off Cluny
Singapore
*Detached House*

See pages 154 to 163

2013–2015
House at Pergam
Singapore
*Semi-Detached House*

2013–2015
House of the Twins
Singapore
*Detached House*
Reconstruction

See pages 164 to 173

2013–2016
House with an Atrium
Singapore
*Detached House*

2013–2014
Hilltops Penthouse Show Unit
Singapore
*Residential Interior*

2013–2016
House with Towers
Singapore
*Good Class Bungalow*

2013–2015
House at Greenleaf
Singapore
*Semi-Detached House*

2013–2015
House at Jalan Ampang
Singapore
*Semi-Detached House*

2013–2016
House at River Valley
Singapore
*Shophouse*

2013–2015
House with Pianos
Singapore
*Semi-Detached House*

2013–2020
Lumi Tropicana
Kuala Lumpur, Malaysia
*Condominium*

2013–2016
House at Sunset IV
Singapore
Detached House

2013–2014
House with Screens
Singapore
*Residential Interior*

2013–Ongoing
House at Widya Chandra II
Jakarta, Indonesia
*Detached House*

2014
Office at Kallang Junction
Singapore
*Commercial Interior*

2014–2016
House with Slots
Singapore
*Terrace House*

See pages 188 to 195

2014–2016
Black and White House
Singapore
*Good Class Bungalow*

2014–2016
House of the Staggered
Blocks
Singapore
*Good Class Bungalow*

2015–2018
Glissando House
Singapore
*Semi-Detached House*

2015–2017
V House
Singapore
*Semi-Detached House*

2015–2021
Hilltops Super Penthouse
Singapore
*Residential Interior*

2015–2016
Hilltops Penthouses I & II
Singapore
*Residential Interiors*

2015–2018
House with Circles
Singapore
*Detached House*

2015–2018
House at Balmoral
Singapore
*Detached House*

2018
House at Sampurna
Singapore
*Good Class Bungalow*

2018–2021
House at Mount Sinai
Singapore
*Semi-Detached House*

2018–2022
House at Trevose II
Singapore
*Detached House*

2018–2022
House off Bukit Timah III
Singapore
*Good Class Bungalow*

2018–Ongoing
Tropicana Genting
Selangor, Malaysia
*Condominium*

2019–Ongoing
House off Stevens
Singapore
*Good Class Bungalow*

2019–Ongoing
House at Vanda V
Singapore
*Detached House*

2019–Ongoing
Opus Bay
Batam, Indonesia
*Mixed-Use Development*

2019–Ongoing
House off Holland
Singapore
*Good Class Bungalow*

2019–Ongoing
House at Hillcrest
Singapore
*Detached House*

2019–Ongoing
House at Hillcrest II
Singapore
*Semi-Detached House*

2019–Ongoing
House off Chancery
Singapore
*Detached House*

2019–2022
House off Farrer II
Singapore
*Detached House*

2019–2022
House off Tanglin
Singapore
*Good Class Bungalow*

2019
A Midsummer's Night Dream
Singapore
*Stage Set*

2019
A 'Home' in Choa Chu Kang
Singapore
*Tombstone*

2020–Ongoing
House at Telok Kurau
Singapore
*Semi-Detached House*

2020–Ongoing
House at Chiltern
Singapore
*Detached House*

2020–Ongoing
House off Farrer III
Singapore
*Semi-Detached House*

2020–Ongoing
House at Pondok Indah III
Jakarta, Indonesia
*Detached House*

2020–Ongoing
House at Leedon
Singapore
*Good Class Bungalow*

2020–Ongoing
House at Holland III
Singapore
*Good Class Bungalow*

2020–Ongoing
House at Novena II
Singapore
*Terrace House*

2020–Ongoing
House at Trevose III
Singapore
*Detached House*

2020–Ongoing
House at Holland IV
Singapore
*Good Class Bungalow*

2020
Shaw Clinic
Singapore
*Commercial Interior*

2020–Ongoing
House off Chancery II
Singapore
*Detached House*

2020–Ongoing
House off Mountbatten III
Singapore
*Detached House*

2020–Ongoing
House at Serangoon Gardens
Singapore
*Semi-Detached House*

2020–Ongoing
House off Bukit Timah IV
Singapore
*Semi-Detached House*

2020–2022
Sentul Pavilion
Kuala Lumpur, Malaysia
*Multi-Purpose Venue*

See pages 300 to 311

2021–Ongoing
House off East Coast Road
Singapore
*Conserved Terrace House*

2021–Ongoing
House at Greenleaf II
Singapore
*Semi-Detached House*

2021–Ongoing
House at Serangoon Gardens II
Singapore
*Semi-Detached House*

2021
=DREAMS Campus at Haig Road
Singapore
*Educational*

2021–Ongoing
House off Bukit Timah V
Singapore
*Semi-Detached House*

2021–Ongoing
House at Sunset V
Singapore
*Detached House*

2021–Ongoing
Houses at Kampung Chantek
Singapore
*Mixed Landed*

2021–Ongoing
House at Choa Chu Kang
Singapore
*Detached House*

2021–Ongoing
House off Bukit Timah VI
Singapore
*Detached House*

2021–Ongoing
House at Leedon II
Singapore
*Good Class Bungalow*

2021–Ongoing
House off Bukit Timah VII
Singapore
*Detached House*

2021–Ongoing
House at Ford II
Singapore
*Good Class Bungalow*

2021–Ongoing
42 South Bridge Road
Singapore
*Conservation Shophouse*

2021–Ongoing
House at Chatsworth Park
Singapore
*Good Class Bungalow*

2021–Ongoing
House at Mount Sinai II
Singapore
*Semi-Detached House*

2021–Ongoing
House at Novena III
Singapore
*Terrace House*

2021
A 'Home' in Nirvana
Memorial Park
Kuala Lumpur, Malaysia
*Tombstone*

2021
A 'Home' in San Diego Hills
Memorial Park
Jakarta, Indonesia
*Tombstone*

2022–Ongoing
House at Watten II
Singapore
*Semi-Detached House*

2022–Ongoing
House at Upper Thomson
Singapore
*Semi-Detached House*

2022–Ongoing
House off Chancery III
Singapore
*Detached House*

2022–Ongoing
House at Balmoral II
Singapore
*Semi-Detached House*

2022–Ongoing
Sanya Residential
Development
Hainan, China
*Condominium*

2022–Ongoing
House at Mayfield
Singapore
*Detached House*

2022–Ongoing
House at West Coast
Singapore
*Detached House*

2022–Ongoing
House at Thomson
Singapore
*Terrace House*

2022–Ongoing
House at Westlake
Singapore
*Detached House*

2022–Ongoing
House at Chiltern
Singapore
*Detached House*

2022–Ongoing
House at Nipis
Singapore
*Semi-Detached House*

2022–Ongoing
House at Tua Kong Green
Singapore
*Terraced House*

2022–Ongoing
House at Tanglin
Singapore
*Good Class Bungalow*

2022–Ongoing
House at Queen Astrid Park
Singapore
*Good Class Bungalow*
*Addition & Alteration*

2022
The Telephone and La Voix
Humaine
Singapore
*Stage Set*

Endnote
1   Good Class Bungalow: see p. 322,
    note 2.

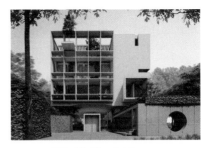

House off Bukit Timah VI
(2021–Ongoing)

House at West Coast
(2022–Ongoing)

House off Chancery III
(2022–Ongoing)

House at Serangoon Gardens
(2020–Ongoing)

House off Chancery II (2020–Ongoing)

House off Bukit Timah V
(2021–Ongoing)

House off Stevens
(2019–Ongoing)

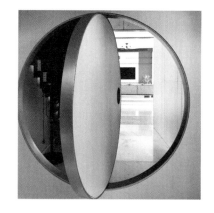

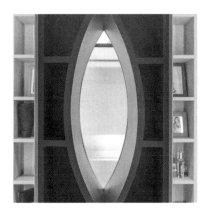

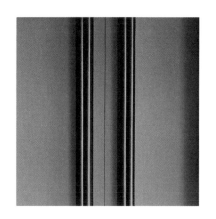
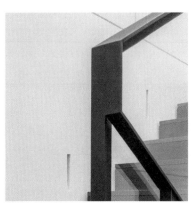

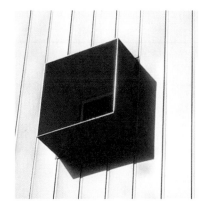

# Awards

President*s Design Award (P*DA), Singapore

2009
Design of the Year (Honourable Mention)
House at Watten, Singapore

2012
Design of the Year (Letter of Commendation)
House in Three Movements, Singapore

2016
Designer of the Year
Rene Tan

Singapore Institute of Architects (SIA)
Architectural Design Awards

2008
Honourable Mention (Residential)
House at Holland, Singapore

2011
Honourable Mention (Residential)
House at Watten, Singapore

2011
Honourable Mention (Residential)
House at Damansara, Kuala Lumpur, Malaysia

2011
Honourable Mention (Commercial)
d7, Kuala Lumpur, Malaysia

2012
Design Award (Residential)
House in Three Movements, Singapore

2012
Honourable Mention (Commercial)
d6, Kuala Lumpur, Malaysia

2013
Design Award (Residential)
Green Collection, Singapore

2013
Honourable Mention (Residential)
Svarga Residence, Bali, Indonesia

2014
Honourable Mention (Residential)
House with Courtyards, Singapore

2015
Design Award (Residential)
House with Bridges, Singapore

2015
SIA Bathroom Design Awards
House with Bridges, Singapore

2016
Design Award (Residential)
House off Cluny, Singapore

2019
Design Award (Residential)
House with a Sanctum, Singapore

2019
Honourable Mention (Residential)
Shorefront, Penang, Malaysia

2020
Design Award (Residential)
Spice Terraces, Singapore

2020
Design Award (Special Category)
A Midsummer's Night Dream Stage Set, Singapore

2020
Merit Award (Special Category)
A 'Home' in Choa Chu Kang, Singapore

2021
Merit Award (Residential)
House with Gables, Singapore

2022
Design Award (Residential)
Petit Jervois, Singapore

Architects Regional Council Asia (ARCASIA)
Awards for Architecture

2014
Gold (Single Family Residential)
Svarga Residence, Bali, Indonesia

2015
Mention (Multiple Family Residential Complexes)
Green Collection, Singapore


Design for Asia Awards, Hong Kong

2017
Bronze
House with Shadows, Singapore


FIABCI World Prix d'Excellence Awards

2022
Gold (World – Residential High Rise)
The Fennel, Kuala Lumpur, Malaysia


Interior Design Confederation Singapore (IDCS)
Design Excellence Awards (IDEA)

2015
Gold (Workplace Design)
Office @ Kallang Junction, Singapore

2015
Gold (Residential)
House with Screens, Singapore

2016
Gold (Asia Pacific, Best Private House)
House with Towers, Singapore

2016
Bronze (Best Residential Kitchen)
House of the Staggered Blocks, Singapore


International Design Awards

2012
Silver
House in Three Movements, Singapore

2012
Bronze
Svarga Residence, Bali, Indonesia


Pertubuhan Akitek Malaysia (PAM) Awards

2011
Gold (Single Residential)
House at Damansara, Kuala Lumpur, Malaysia

2011
Silver (Overseas)
House at Watten, Singapore

2011
Silver (Commercial)
d7, Kuala Lumpur, Malaysia

2011
Commendation (Overseas)
House at Kebayoran Bahru, Jakarta, Indonesia

2012
Silver (Overseas)
House in Three Movements, Singapore

2012
Commendation (Commercial)
d6, Kuala Lumpur, Malaysia

PropertyGuru Asia Pacific Awards

2018
Best Condo Development (Klang Valley)
The Fennel, Kuala Lumpur, Malaysia

2018
Best Condo Development (Malaysia)
The Fennel, Kuala Lumpur, Malaysia


Tatler Design Awards

2018
Best Multi-Generational Project
House of Generations, Singapore

2021
Best Architectural Concept
Spice Terraces


Chicago Athenaeum International Architecture Awards

2016
Winner
The Capers, Kuala Lumpur, Malaysia


Urban Redevelopment Authority Architectural
Heritage Awards, Singapore

2011
Winner (Category B)
House at Cable, Singapore


Urban Redevelopment Authority 20 Under 45 Awards,
Singapore

2017
Jonathan Quek Shao Sheng


World Architectural Festival Awards

2012
Shortlisted (Future Projects – Residential)
Svarga Residence, Bali Indonesia

2015
Shortlisted (New and Old)
House of the Connoisseur, Singapore

2016
Shortlisted (Future Projects – Residential)
Shorefront, Penang, Malaysia

2017
Shortlisted
The Capers, Kuala Lumpur, Malaysia

2017
Shortlisted
House with Shadows, Singapore

2018
Shortlisted
The Fennel, Kuala Lumpur, Malaysia

2021
Shortlisted
Spice Terraces, Singapore

2021
Shortlisted
House with Two Faces, Singapore

2021
Shortlisted
A 'Home' in Choa Chu Kang, Singapore

2022
Shortlisted (Temporary/Meanwhile Uses)
Le Corbusier: The Travelling Exhibition

# Studio

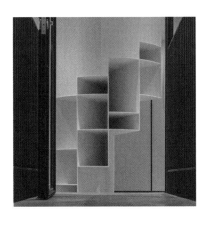

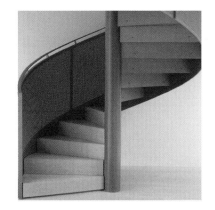

# Project Credits

**House at Holland**
Project team: Rene Tan, TK Quek, Faye Moey
Civil and structural engineer: MSE Consultants
Mechanical and electrical engineer: Elead Associates
Quantity surveyor: KH Lim Quantity Surveyors
Main contractor: Chen Guan Builders

**House at Watten**
Project team: Rene Tan, Jes Ang
Civil and structural engineer: Wong Chi Keong
    in collaboration with MSE Consultants
Mechanical and electrical engineer: E3 Consulting Engineers
Quantity surveyor: PQS Consultants
Main contractor: Join-Aim

**Double 'C' House**
Project team: Rene Tan, TK Quek, Chua Z-Chian
Civil and structural engineer: MSE Consultants
Mechanical and electrical engineer: AE&T Consultants
Quantity surveyor: PQS Consultants
Main contractor: Sil-Bright Construction

**House at Damansara**
Project team: Rene Tan
Architect in association: F H Loo Arkitek
Main contractor: Megabena Teras

**House at Cable**
Project team: Rene Tan, TK Quek, Angeline Yoo, Jes Ang
Civil and structural engineer: BKG Consultants
Mechanical and electrical engineer: E3 Consulting Engineers
Quantity surveyor: HY M&E Consultancy Services
Main contractor: Huat Builders

**House at Pondok Indah**
Project team: Rene Tan, Jonathan Quek
Civil and structural engineer: Rudy Mulyana and team
Mechanical and electrical engineer: Rudy Mulyana and team
Quantity surveyor: Rudy Mulyana and team
Main contractor: Rudy Mulyana and team

**House in Three Movements**
Project team: Rene Tan, TK Quek, Chua Z-Chian, Jes Ang
Civil and structural engineer: PTS Consultants
Quantity surveyor: PQS Consultants
Main contractor: Renown Builders

**Shorefront**
Project team: Rene Tan, TK Quek, Eddie Gan, Fiona Tan
Architect in association: SM Ooi Architect
Civil and structural engineer: Perunding YSL in collaboration
    with YTL Design Group
Mechanical and electrical engineer: JPR in collaboration
    with YTL Design Group
Quantity surveyor: Syarikat Pembinaan YTL
Main contractor: Syarikat Pembinaan YTL

**Sentul East**
Project team: Rene Tan, TK Quek, Eddie Gan, Han Yee Kwang
Civil and structural engineer: Perunding YSL
    in collaboration with YTL Design Group
Mechanical and electrical engineer: Perunding K L Chock
    in collaboration with YTL Design Group
Quantity surveyor: YTL Design Group
Main contractor: Syarikat Pembinaan YTL
Landscape architect: Seksan Design

**Svarga Residence**
Project team: Rene Tan
Mechanical and electrical engineer: Paul Tandean
Main contractor: Paul Tandean

**House on a Prairie**
Project team: Rene Tan, TK Quek, Jonathan Quek, Jes Ang
Civil and structural engineer: PTS Consultants
Mechanical and electrical engineer: Elead Associates
Quantity surveyor: WS Surveyorship
Main contractor: OAL Builders

**House of the Connoisseur**
Project team: Rene Tan, TK Quek, Charles Wee, Kristine Cruz
Civil and structural engineer: E123 Consultants
Mechanical and electrical engineer: LAC Engineers
    & Associates
Quantity surveyor: WS Surveyorship
Main contractor: C+S Builders

**Art Collector's House**
Project team: TK Quek, Jonathan Quek, Charles Wee, Jes Ang
Civil and structural engineer: PTS Consultants
Quantity surveyor: PQS Consultants
Main contractor: Builders Trends

**House with Bridges**
Project team: Rene Tan, TK Quek, Koh Kai Li, Kristine Cruz
Civil and structural engineer: PTS Consultants
Mechanical and electrical engineer: LAC Engineers & Associates
Quantity surveyor: WS Surveyorship
Main contractor: Builders Trends

**House off Cluny**
Project team: Rene Tan, TK Quek, Koh Sock Mui, Kristine Cruz
Civil and structural engineer: E123 Consultants
Mechanical and electrical engineer: AE&T Consultants
Quantity surveyor: WS Surveyorship
Main contractor: Guan Tong Construction Co.

**House of the Twins**
Project team: Rene Tan, TK Quek, Fiona Tan, Jes Ang
Civil and structural engineer: PTS Consultants
Mechanical and electrical engineer: AE&T Consultants
Quantity surveyor: WS Surveyorship
Main contractor: Huat Builders

**House with Shadows**
Project team: Rene Tan, TK Quek, Melvin Keng, Jes Ang
Civil and structural engineer: PTS Consultants
Mechanical and electrical engineer: AE&T Consultants
Quantity surveyor: WS Surveyorship
Main contractor: Builders Trends

**House with Slots**
Project team: Rene Tan, TK Quek,
    Pornpailin Krittayapirom (Ploy), Jes Ang
Civil and structural engineer: PTS Consultants
Quantity surveyor: WS Surveyorship
Main contractor: Builders 265

**Meshed Up House**
Project team: Rene Tan, Suarpha Vangvasu (Jaa), Charles Wee,
    Kristine Cruz
Civil and structural engineer: JS Tan Consultants
Mechanical and electrical engineer: LAC Engineers & Associates
Quantity surveyor: Oliver Ho & Associates
Main contractor: Soon Thong Construction

**House with a Sanctum**
Project team: Rene Tan, Koh Sock Mui, Kristine Cruz
Civil and structural engineer: PTS Consultants
Mechanical and electrical engineer: HPX Consulting Engineers
Quantity surveyor: WS Surveyorship
Main contractor: Shinhan Tech-Engineering

**House with a Roof**
Project team: Rene Tan, TK Quek, Koh Kai Li, Jes Ang
Civil and structural engineer: PTS Consultants
Mechanical and electrical engineer: HPX Consulting Engineers
Quantity surveyor: WS Surveyorship
Main contractor: Berjaya Buildcon

**House with Two Faces**
Project team: Rene Tan, TK Quek, Huang Wei, Jes Ang
Civil and structural engineer: TNJ Consultants & Partners
Mechanical and electrical engineer: HPX Consulting Engineers
Quantity surveyor: WS Surveyorship
Main contractor: Builders Trends

**House with Twin Gardens**
Project team: Rene Tan, TK Quek, Allan Tongol, Jes Ang
Civil and structural engineer: TNJ Consultants & Partners
Mechanical and electrical engineer: LAC Engineers & Associates
Quantity surveyor: Oliver Ho & Associates
Main contractor: Berjaya Buildcon

**House with Gables**
Project team: Rene Tan, TK Quek, Jonathan Quek, Meris Ng,
    Jes Ang
Civil and structural engineer: TNJ Consultants & Partners
Mechanical and electrical engineer: CCA & Partners
Quantity surveyor: WS Surveyorship
Main contractor: Sinwah-APAC Construction

**House with an Oculus**
Project team: Rene Tan, TK Quek, Dongsuk Lee, Koh Kai Li, Jes Ang
Civil and structural engineer: TNJ Consultants & Partners
Mechanical and electrical engineer: LAC Engineers & Associates
Quantity surveyor: WS Surveyorship
Main contractor: Daiya Engineering & Construction

**Petit Jervois**
Project team: Rene Tan, Tiw Pek Hong, Koh Sock Mui, Melvin Keng,
    Dongsuk Lee, Jes Ang
Civil and structural engineer: TW-Asia Consultants
Mechanical and electrical engineer: United Project Consultants
Quantity surveyor: Threesixty Cost Management
Main contractor: Daiya Engineering & Construction

**Spice Terraces**
Project team: Rene Tan, Natalie Mok, Eunice Lim,
    Suarpha Vangvasu (Jaa), Jes Ang
Civil and structural engineer: MSE Consultants
Main contractor: Huat Builders

**House of Terracing Courtyards**
Project team: Rene Tan, TK Quek, Koh Kai Li, Jes Ang
Civil and structural engineer: PTS Consultants
Mechanical and electrical engineer: LAC Engineers & Associates
Quantity surveyor: WS Surveyorship
Main contractor: U.Sage Contracts

**Sentul Pavilion**
Project team: Rene Tan, Jonathan Quek, Eunice Lim
Architect in association: E'Kuan Architect
Civil and structural engineer: Perunding YSL
Landscape architect: Praxcis Design
Interior design: YTL Construction

RT+Q Architects have made all reasonable efforts to credit the parties involved correctly. If there are any unintentional omissions or errors, please contact us so that we may update our records accordingly.

# Photographic Credits

**Albert Lim**
14–15, 18–25, 28–29, 50–51, 53 (middle), 54–61, 64–71, 74–77, 82 (top), 83, 86 (bottom), 88–89, 92, 94–99, 102–103, 106–107, 109, 111–113, 140 (top), 144–146, 148–149, 152–153, 164–165, 168–173, 204–205, 207–209, 212–217, 315 (right), 318, 332–333, 338–339

**Ed Simon**
132–134, 136–137, 141–143

**Fabian Ong**
238–239, 242–247

**Fifoto**
42–43, 46–49

**K Studio**
34

**Masano Kawana**
30–32, 35–37, 40–41, 78–79, 81, 82 (bottom), 84–85, 86 (top), 87, 110, 114–115, 118–125, 128–131, 154–156, 158–159, 162–163, 174–176, 178–181, 184–189, 192–195, 198–199, 202–203, 218–220, 224–229, 231–232, 233 (top), 234–237, 248–253, 256–262, 266–269, 272–273, 275–276, 278–282, 284–285, 288 (left), 289 (right), 290, 291 (left and top right), 292–295, 298–301, 304–311, 314 (left), 315 (left), 332–333, 338–339, 348–352

**New Opera Singapore**
314 (right)

All images © RT+Q Architects unless otherwise stated above.

# Acknowledgments

This book would not have been possible without the clients who have trusted us to realize their ideal homes through the years, our colleagues past and present, and our collaborators and supporters near and far for the last twenty years.

Construction is a process that takes years or even decades. This book has similarly been more than five years in the making and owes its final realization to the patient and consistent efforts of editor Justin, and writer Jingmei. They have shepherded the idea of a monograph through to fruition by studying our work, asking questions and prodding us to collect all the disparate data from multiple sources for consolidation in printed form. Hanson has been key in distilling the mountain of material into this beautifully laid-out book.

We would also like to thank our publishers, Thames & Hudson, for their faith in the value and appeal of our work. In particular, we would like to thank Augusta Pownall for her insights and guidance through the whole process.

In addition, we would like to thank our following colleagues: Sock Mui, for giving up a portion of her sanity to make this happen; Liane, for ensuring that two million lines and two billion leaves are drawn; Naz, for trawling our archives and records for the information necessary for the compilation of a monograph; and Jesline for running the office since 2003.

Such a longstanding project is built on the efforts of not just the current team but those who have contributed to the book over the years. We would like to take this opportunity to acknowledge and thank them for their efforts as well.

—Rene & TK

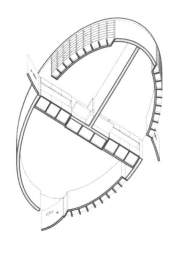

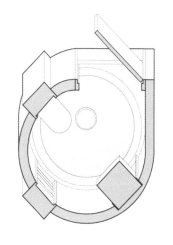

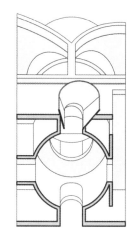

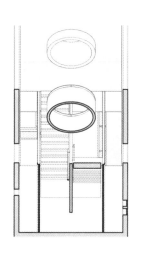

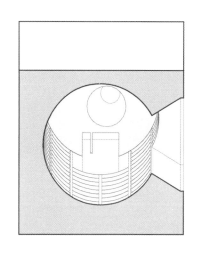

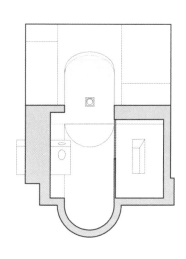

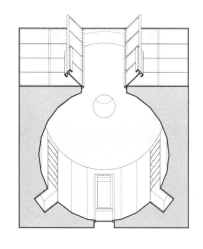

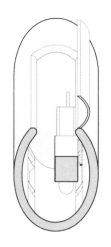

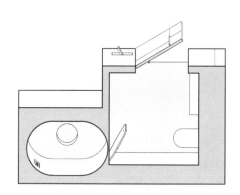

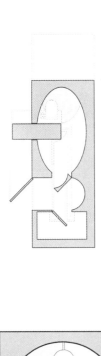
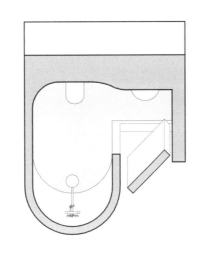
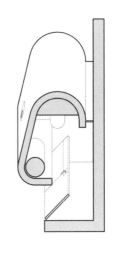
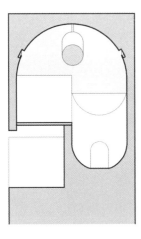
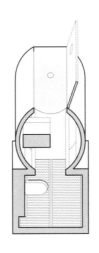
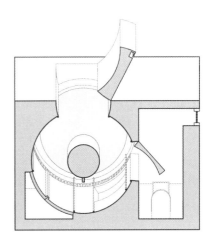
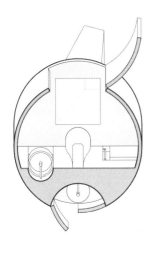
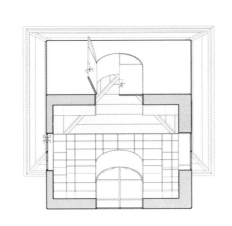
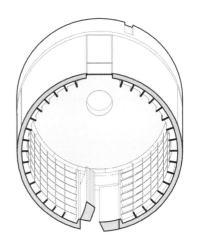

# Contributors

**Chan Sau Yan, Sonny** was born in 1941 in Kuala Lumpur. He studied in London at the Northern Polytechnic and the Architectural Association School of Architecture. He established his own practice in 1993 after twenty-nine years at Kumpulan Akitek, Singapore. He was an external examiner and adjunct associate professor at the National University of Singapore. In 2011, he was awarded the President*s Design Award Designer of the Year. In 2013, he published his monograph *Green Ink on an Envelope*, documenting his architectural journey over four decades.

**Kelley Cheng** is the founder and creative director of design studio The Press Room, a publishing and design consultancy, and Studio SML, a design documentary platform. Trained as an architect, she is also an external examiner at the National University of Singapore School of Architecture and a visiting professor at the China Academy of Art, Hangzhou. Kelley is a frequent name on international design judging panels, including Red Dot Awards, Nagoya-Do!, Design for Asia Award, Creative Circle Award and James Dyson Award. In 2019, the National Design Centre presented her twenty-year retrospective exhibition 'Proportion & Emotion: 20 years in Design with Kelley Cheng', and in 2020 she was awarded the SkillsFuture Fellowship and the prestigious President*s Design Award Designer of the Year, both presented by the president of Singapore.

**Luo Jingmei** is a Singaporean writer and editor. The architect by training spent her formative working years at award-winning firm ipli Architects. She is a former deputy editor of *Cubes Indesign*, and her articles have appeared in publications and websites such as *Vogue Living*, *Vogue Singapore*, *Robb Report*, *Design + Architecture*, *Portfolio*, *Sleeper*, *Habitus*, *Dwell*, *Indesign*, *Design Anthology*, *Channel News Asia Luxury*, *Surface Asia*, *Tatler Homes*, *Interior Design* and the Design Society. Jingmei also has experience shaping editorial content for architecture firms. She seeks to author authentic narratives and is passionate about finding meaning in built form and exploring how buildings impact their users.

**Mok Wei Wei** is the principal of W Architects, a Singapore-based practice with a critically acclaimed body of work. He studied at the National University of Singapore and is an honorary professor of his alma mater. Over the years, he has served as a statutory board member of multiple planning agencies, and actively contributes to the urban planning of Singapore.

**Robert Powell** is an architect, city planner, author/editor and critic. He was, from January 2016 until November 2019, Professor of Architecture at Taylor's University, Selangor, Malaysia. Previously, he was Associate Professor of Architecture at the National University of Singapore (1984 to 2000). He is the author/editor of over forty books, mainly on the architecture of Southeast Asia.

**Lillian Tay** trained as an engineer and architect at Princeton, where she first met the young Rene Tan. She worked at KPF, New York, before returning to Kuala Lumpur, where she has been a director at VERITAS Architects since 1995. Lillian is a past president of the Malaysian Institute of Architects (PAM).

**Erwin Viray** currently leads the Sustainability Initiatives at the Singapore University of Technology and Design. Prior to his current role, he was the head of Architecture and Sustainable Design Pillar from May 2016 to July 2021. Erwin was Global Excellence Professor at Kyoto Institute of Technology and head of the Graduate School of Architecture and Design from 2012 to 2016, and Chief Communications Officer for Kyoto Design Lab. He served as a board member of the TOTO Gallery MA in Tokyo and a member of the Advisory Council for the Barcelona Institute of Architecture. Erwin is an Award Ambassador for the LafargeHolcim Awards in Asia Pacific and has served as a jury chair and member of various prominent architecture awards in the region. Erwin has also been an editor of the influential magazine *a+u: Architecture + Urbanism* since 1996 and has authored several books and numerous articles for specialized journals and architectural magazines.

**Alexander Wong** is an award-winning architect and writer based in Hong Kong. After gaining a postgraduate degree at Princeton University, he established his own design firm, Alexander Wong Architects, in 2001, which has won more than seventy major international design awards. His published works include *Naked + White* (2005) and *ARCHIPHANTASY* (2021).

House with an Oculus (pp. 260–267)

351